Are We French Yet?

Keith & Val's Adventures in Provence

Keith Van Sickle

Published by Dresher Publishing, Menlo Park, California.
Printed in the United States

ISBN 978-0-9983120-5-7

First Edition

Cover design by Teddi Black
Illustrations by Anthony Genilo

To my sister Sherry

ALSO BY KEITH VAN SICKLE

When the Good Lord begins to
doubt the world, he remembers
that he created Provence.

Frédéric Mistral

Table of Contents

Not Quite What I Planned

Val and I couldn't wait to get back to France. For weeks, we had been packing our bags and cleaning our house in preparation for our three-month trip abroad. Getting ready for springtime in Provence is a complicated affair, and even though we've done it many times, it never gets easier.

Finally, just three days before our flight, we'd worked through most of our long checklist and had some free time on our hands. Whenever we are about to go on a long trip like this I get nervous—not the worried kind of nervous but rather the excited-and-can't-wait-to-get-going kind of nervous. I started pacing around the house.

"You look like you need something to do," said Val. "Let's go for a bike ride out on Old Page Mill Road. We can get some exercise before we have to sit on a plane all day."

"Good idea!" I said. Except it wasn't.

We like to ride on Old Page Mill because it's a quiet road with hardly any cars. It's shady and has gentle hills, which is perfect for us because we're not serious bikers. In fact, we're kind of slow. I can't count the times I've been passed by riders on expensive bikes, wearing their sleek outfits, while I poke along in my baggy shorts and old polo shirt.

It was a quiet day so I let my mind wander as we pedaled along. Val sometimes accuses me of being, um, inattentive, and this time she was definitely right. I started thinking about what to have for dinner when we got to France—should it be *coq au vin* or *daube de boeuf*? No, I thought, I'll have my favorite, *confit de canard*.

I was dreamily savoring that first bite of crispy duck when a squirrel darted in front of me. I didn't see it until it was too late and I slammed on the brakes, which only made a bad situation worse. The front tire locked up and I went flying over the handlebars. The next thing I knew I was lying on the ground and my right wrist hurt. A lot.

Val ran over to me. "Are you ok?" she said, a panicked look on her face.

"I'm still in one piece," I said, "but my wrist really hurts. I think we'd better go to the hospital."

We spent the rest of the afternoon in the emergency room, waiting our turn while my wrist throbbed and I worried about our trip to Provence. Would we have to cancel it? We had already paid for our flight and rental car, plus the house we would be staying in for three months. If I couldn't travel, could we get our money back?

Then there was medical care. Would I be able to get what I needed in France? What about physical therapy? And would our insurance pay for it?

Even if we could still go to France, I wouldn't be 100% when we got there. I hadn't hurt my legs so I could still walk, but if my wrist was broken would I be able to drive?

You have a lot of time to fret when you're in a waiting room.

A nurse eventually called my name and X-rays confirmed the worst—a broken wrist that would take two months to heal. Next I saw a doctor who put a cast on my hand and lower arm and told me to come back in a month for a checkup.

"I'm sorry," I said, "but I can't because I'll be in France then."

"That's fine," he said, "French doctors are excellent. Just make an appointment with a hand specialist there. And be sure to do physical therapy after the bone heals."

"Right," I thought, "like that's going to be easy." I didn't know much about the French health care system, so finding a specialized doctor and therapist was a daunting challenge. This definitely wasn't the fun start to our trip that I had been hoping for.

The Interrogation

Three days after I broke my wrist, Val and I set off for France with our suitcases plus our dog and her crate. Schlepping all that gear is tough enough without a broken bone and here I was one-armed and practically useless (or as Val would say, "More useless than usual.")

Luckily, a friend drove us to the airport and helped carry our bags to the check-in counter. And Val had the presence of mind to reserve a porter to help us when our flight landed in Europe. But she still had to do most of the work and hasn't let me forget it. She claims that it gave her "brownie points for life" and she gleefully redeems them whenever she gets the chance.

Once we settled into our place in Provence, it was time to track down that doctor.

"How do I find one?" I asked Val. "They don't have Yellow Pages here. And what do you even call somebody like that?" It's not like "hand specialist" was in our French dictionary (I checked).

"Let's ask Sophie," suggested Val. "She always knows what to do."

That was a good idea. Sophie and her husband Jacques are friends of ours so I called her, making sure to look up a few words first so I could explain what had happened. You never know when you'll have the opportunity to expand your vocabulary and this time it was *percuter* (to crash), *cassé* (broken) and *radius* (radius bone).

Sophie, as always, came to the rescue. By the next day she had found a hand specialist at a nearby clinic and made an appointment for me. The clinic was called *SOS Main* (SOS Hand), which didn't sound very medical to me—it sounded more like what you use to wave in distress. Not sure what to expect, Val decided to join me and off to the clinic we went.

We arrived well before my appointment and it was a good thing we did because I was told I needed a French X-ray. I had brought the one taken in the US but for some reason it wasn't good enough, so I was sent downstairs to the X-ray center where I waited in line with about a dozen other people. When it was finally my turn I tried to be helpful and told the technician that I had *cassé le fin de mon radius* (broken the end of my radius bone), pointing to where the break was.

She looked at me like I was a two-year-old. "*Ce n'est pas le fin du radius, c'est l'extrémité,*" she said (It's not the *end* of the radius bone, it's the *extremity*).

"Sheesh," I thought, "is there really such a big difference?" I was reminded yet again how precise the French are with their language.

After the X-ray, Val and I headed up for my appointment with the doctor. It did not start well.

In the US, back in the old days, doctors were kind of like gods. They told you what to do and you did it. You never questioned a doctor and you certainly didn't suggest treatments based on your Internet research or something your neighbor told you. It's still like that in France—Me Important Doctor, you lowly patient.

The doctor introduced himself as Dr. Selemi and formally shook hands with us because the French just love to shake hands. My handshake was awkward and left-handed due to my broken right wrist but it was important that we follow protocol. Then the doctor started aggressively asking me questions in French. I would barely start to answer one question and he would launch into another.

"When was your accident? No, *exactly* when?"

"How did this happen?"

"Why didn't you avoid the squirrel? They are quite small, you know."

"Why didn't you have surgery? I would have operated on your wrist immediately. What's wrong with your American doctor?"

After I answered his questions in a suitably deferential fashion and showed that I could sort of speak French, the doctor started to mellow. Then he threw me a curveball.

"How many states have you visited in America?"

Where did that come from? I was so startled by the question that it took me a moment to answer. "Uh...er...um...maybe half," I finally stammered.

"I've been to 43!" he said proudly.

To my surprise, I learned that Dr. Selemi is a huge fan of the US. He fell in love with the country as a high school exchange student and now vacations there every year. AND he speaks English way better than I speak French. So I could have avoided a lot of heartburn if he had just conducted his interrogation in English.

I must have passed his test because he suddenly became very friendly. The French can be formal and even aloof at first but we got past that quickly. We started chatting and I asked if he had ever visited my home state of California.

"Of course," he said. "I've been to Disneyland, Yosemite, San Francisco, and lots of other places. My favorite is Napa Valley because I love wine."

"Oh, me too," I said, "and the ones from around here are my favorites."

"Really?" he said, then paused and looked thoughtful for a moment. "Well you know, I have a friend..."

It turns out that this friend owns a winery in nearby Châteauneuf-du-Pape, one of the most famous wine towns in the world. Dr. Selemi excused himself to make a phone call and the next thing we knew we were invited to a private tasting on the following Sunday.

This was one of those "Toto, I don't think we're in Kansas any more" moments. Somehow, some way, in just a few minutes I'd gone from being an idiot who couldn't avoid an itty-bitty squirrel to being invited to a famous winery. With a doctor I'd just met!

As we drove home after the appointment, Val looked at me and said, "This would *never* happen back home."

Doctor's Orders

Châteauneuf-du-Pape means "the Pope's new chateau" because his summer palace had once been there. This was back in the 14th century, when the papacy moved from Rome to nearby Avignon for about a hundred years. The ruins of the famous chateau still tower over the countryside, surrounded by mile after mile of what had once been papal vineyards. It was early spring on the day of our wine tasting and the vines were beginning to bud, creating a sea of bright green in all directions.

We were allowed to bring two friends so we invited Sophie and Jacques—he's one of my wine buddies and was thrilled because it's not every day you get a private tasting at a top *domaine*. On Sunday morning, church bells ringing, we all met in the town's main square.

"Dr. Selemi," I said, "I'd like to introduce you to Sophie and Jacques."

"Oh please, call me Elyas," he said, shaking their hands. "There's no reason to be stuffy." So now we were on a first-name basis!

It was a beautiful day—the sky was blue, the air was crisp and we were ready to taste some seriously good wine. By luck, that day was also the town's annual wine fair and Elyas had generously bought us tickets.

The fair was held in the town's community center, a big, plain room that you could imagine being used for Bingo games on a Tuesday night. But now it was filled with row after row of foldup tables. Every winemaker in town was there, each of them standing behind a table covered with bottles of wine, while people milled around in the aisles. All you had to do was walk up to a table and stick out your glass for a pour of some of the best wine in the world. The whole affair was informal and friendly, not a wine snob in sight.

"I think I'm in heaven," said Jacques.

"Thank goodness," I said, "that I can still drink wine with my left hand!"

As we worked our way through the room, swirling and sipping, Elyas kept making introductions—to his family, his friends, his friends' friends, winemakers he knew, people from the village, it went on and on. After a couple of hours, our heads were spinning from all that sipping and we decided to break for lunch. We went to the food hall where Elyas introduced us to Françoise, the owner of the winery and the host of our private tasting. We all chatted together over lunch and when it was over, Elyas surprised us by deciding to go home.

"I've had enough wine for today and need to stop," he said. "Doctor's orders!"

That left the four of us with Françoise, who was not only the owner of the winery—the seventh generation in her family—but also its chief winemaker and the president of the local women's winemaking association. She was talented and accomplished and remarkably generous with her time, spending hours with us, people she barely knew.

First she drove us to her winery outside of town, where she gave us a tour and an explanation of every step of the winemaking process. We saw the places where her workers brought in the grapes, sorted them, crushed them, separated out the juice and let it ferment into wine, then bottled it and shipped it to customers around the world. The best part was when she took us down to the cellar to taste some young wine. The *cave* was chilly and dark.

Françoise turned a tap on one of the gigantic barrels and filled a glass. "Here," she said, "try this and tell me what you think."

What did I think? I thought it was dark and delicious and a bit mysterious because it was still evolving. We went from one barrel to the next, tasting the wine from each and comparing them. Françoise tasted along with us, explaining how she planned to take a little of this one and a little of that one to come up with the perfect blend for the next year's wines.

Jacques and I had visited wineries before but never received the royal treatment like this. It was a kind of master class in winemaking and we were such enthusiastic students that I think Françoise enjoyed it as much as we did.

After the winery tour, we went back to her tasting room in town to try more wines, older ones, and Françoise explained to us how they changed over time.

Finally—late afternoon now—it was time to say our goodbyes. We had shaken hands when first introduced, but our time together had somehow broken down a barrier so now it was kisses on the cheek all around, left-right-left in the local style. As Sophie, Jacques, Val and I walked contentedly, if a bit unsteadily, back to our cars, we marveled at what a magical day it had been.

Magical, that's the right word. Magic seems to happen to us in France.

From Switzerland To France

There's no other way to say it: Val and I are in love with France. And our love affair began, strangely enough, in Switzerland.

In mid-career, my company offered me an assignment in that land of cows and chocolate. It was intriguing because there's nothing Val and I like better than traveling to foreign countries. But could we actually live in one?

"Do they speak English there?" Val asked.

"No," I said, "Switzerland has four national languages but none of them is English."

"Hm."

But it was a rare opportunity and the more we thought about it the better we liked the idea. Val looked for a job near mine and when she found one we decided that this was meant to be. So we packed our bags and moved to Neuchâtel, in the French-speaking part of the country. We spent five years there and it changed our lives.

Switzerland introduced to a whole new way of living, where your job didn't dominate your life like it did in California. Yes, the Swiss work hard but they also take four weeks of vacation every year. And they never, ever work on Sunday.

One day Val came home from work and said, "I got in trouble today."

"What happened?" I said. "Are you ok?"

"It was a busy day so I was having a quick sandwich at my desk for lunch," she explained. "Then Jean-Marc came by and told me I needed to take a proper lunch break. He kind of lectured me and told me that I had to take time away from my desk because sitting there all day is 'unhealthy.'"

Val and I have spent most of our careers in the so-called Silicon Valley, near San Francisco, where people work all the time and even a quick sandwich at your desk is sometimes a luxury. "Wow," I said, "can you imagine someone saying that back home?" It was shocking at first, but over time we came to appreciate how those vacations and lunch breaks and quiet Sundays refreshed us and gave us new energy for our jobs.

We used our weekends and vacations to travel all over Europe and everywhere we went we saw that special something the French call *joie de vivre.* People seemed to enjoy life, balancing their work and their free time in a way we didn't back home in the US. We would see them lingering over a glass of wine in a café or sharing a long meal with friends and be envious, so we tried to embrace the "European lifestyle" as best we could.

But all good things come to an end and eventually so did our expat assignment. We reluctantly moved home and plunged back into our busy American lives. While it was wonderful to be with our family and old friends again, it also seemed like something was missing. Europe had been so fascinating! There was history everywhere, like the 10th century abbey in our Swiss village. And every country had a different language and culture and cuisine.

"It's like life there was in color," Val said sadly one day, "and now it's in black and white."

We knew that we had been lucky to live abroad—how many people have that opportunity? We dreamed of doing it again. From time to time we would check job postings to try and find another expat assignment but never had any luck.

Then Val had a crazy idea. We were lying in bed early one Saturday morning when she suddenly sat up.

"I've got it!" she said. "To heck with trying to find a new expat gig. Let's invent our own!"

"What are you talking about?" I replied, still groggy.

"You need a special visa to work in another country," she said, "but that's only if you live there all the time. Let's be part-time expats instead and split our time between two countries."

She stopped and frowned. "We just have to figure out how to earn a living."

"Um, ok" I said. "Can we have some coffee first?"

Over the next few weeks we discussed her idea again and again, and it seemed less crazy the more we talked about it. After many long conversations we finally came up with a plan. Life is short, we decided, so why not try?

"We've been working and saving money for years," Val said, "telling ourselves that 'someday' we'll travel more. Well, maybe someday is *now!*"

Our plan was to quit our jobs and become consultants. This would allow us to work a lot when we were in the US and not so much when we were abroad. The idea of setting our own hours was appealing, as was working for ourselves rather than for The Man, but giving up steady paychecks? That was scary.

Val is the brave one in the family so she went first. She quit her job and developed a group of clients, while I kept my job so we could still pay our bills. Then it was my turn. It was terrifying to take such a leap after decades of steady employment. But off I jumped and found a new career as a consultant.

Next we had to decide where to live. We checked on a government website and learned that we could stay for up to 90 days in nearly any European country without needing a special visa.

"How about Switzerland?" Val said. "We loved living there."

"Of course we did," I replied, "because we had Swiss paychecks and didn't notice how expensive it was. Now there's no way we can afford it on our own. How about Italy? It's a lot cheaper than Switzerland and the food is fantastic."

"Italy's one of my favorite places to go on vacation," she said, "but I'm not sure about staying there a long time. It isn't exactly the most organized place in the world—remember the time it took all day at the post office just to mail a box home?"

"Good point."

We decided to try France because we had been there a lot and always enjoyed it (Neuchâtel is right next to France). It has many things we like, especially the food and wine—that's important if you're going to live in a place for three months. And it's so dense with history and culture and fascinating places to visit, from cathedrals and museums to soaring mountains and glitzy beaches, that we're never bored there.

Once we decided on France we had to pick a town. We planned to go in the springtime, when much of country is still cold, so that pointed us to the south. We thought about Provence, in the far south, because every time we had visited we had enjoyed it so much that it was hard to leave. And it's a rural area with mostly small towns (we're not big-city people) so we figured we could find a nice place to stay. Plus it's so full of charming villages and natural beauty that you feel like you're in the middle of a postcard when you're there. So Provence it was.

We found a house to rent near the town of St-Rémy-de-Provence and had a wonderful time during our first three-month stay. Then, over the next few years, we tried out other parts of Provence (it's a big place). One year we spent our three months near Avignon, another year near Aix-en-Provence, and after comparing the different areas we picked a favorite. We went back to where we started, St-Rémy, and now we go there every spring.

St-Rémy is perfect for us because it's large enough to have a variety of shops and restaurants, yet small enough that we can walk across it in a few minutes. It has a rich history as the town where the medieval seer Nostradamus was born and Vincent Van Gogh painted masterpieces like *Starry Night*. It sits at the foot of the Alpilles Mountains so it's easy to find gorgeous places to hike and bike. And there are things to explore all around St-Rémy, like the ruins of Roman cities and the ancient fortresses perched on rocky mountaintops.

Best of all is St-Rémy's Wednesday market, one of the biggest in Provence. It starts in the center of the old part of town, with vendors selling fresh produce, olives, wine, honey, lavender, colorful tablecloths and everything Provençal under the shade of the big plane trees. From there it spreads out along the town's winding, narrow, cobblestone streets and spills onto the ring road, the one that follows the path of the old ramparts that protected St-Rémy in the Middle Ages. Then it jumps across the road and fills the town's parking lot, with stands selling clothing and knickknacks. We make sure to go early to avoid the crowds, then stop and have a coffee at our favorite café before lugging our bags of goodies back to our place.

Our American friends joke about us spending so much time in France, calling me *Monsieur Frenchy* and teasing Val about her fondness for scarves. And sometimes, in a wistful moment, they'll say, "You two are living the dream." It makes me stop and think, what does that really mean?

I guess that for them it's fresh baguettes and rosé wine and golden fields of sunflowers, but for us it's much more. We don't want to just enjoy an extended vacation, we want to live in France more deeply than we did in Switzerland. We want to have a real connection and become part of a community.

We missed a big opportunity in Switzerland. Yes, we had hiked in the Alps and gone to all of the festivals in our village. And we had made friends, good friends that we still see to this day. But we had only been able to skim the surface of Swiss society because we hadn't learned the local language, French.

Val had gotten good enough to stammer her way through a simple conversation but no more, while I was inept, able to order at a restaurant and not much else. So while we could say hello to our neighbors we couldn't have an in-depth conversation. We couldn't read the local paper or watch TV. When there was an election we couldn't understand what the issues were. It was as if we were separated from the real Switzerland by a pane of glass, able to see but not touch.

We resolved that it would be different in France. This time, we wanted to immerse ourselves in the country. We wanted to understand the culture and its complex social codes. We wanted to dive into French history and literature and follow the political battles of the day. We wanted to meet all kinds of French people, not just the ones who happened to speak English, and be able to see the world through their eyes. More than anything, we wanted to make France a real home. And maybe become a little French ourselves.

We made progress during our first couple of years, taking French classes when we were in the US and meeting with language partners when we were in Provence. We learned French well enough to read books (slowly) and watch TV. We were able to have meaningful conversations, even though we sometimes had to stop and figure out how to express an idea with our limited vocabularies. Best of all, we made a wonderful circle of French friends, like Sophie and Jacques. Spending time with them, and involving ourselves in the day-to-day life of St-Rémy, made us feel like we were becoming part of a community.

But there was still a lot of work ahead before we would feel French, and the key was mastering the language. We had gotten to the point where we were kind of competent, but we knew that to go much further we needed an expert to help us.

Enter Geneviève.

Parlez-vous Français?

It's All About The Tongue

During our first couple of years in Provence, Val and I kept hunting for a good French class to take. We wanted one with only a few students, where each person received lots of attention, but all the classes we found were big and impersonal. Then someone told us about a nearby language school with a professor who gave private lessons on the side, which is how we met Geneviève.

Geneviève is a native of the area and grew up in a village—a hamlet really—of just a few hundred people. She still lives in the house where she was born, a rambling place with a big garden, and this is where she holds her private classes.

She has red hair and a calm manner, and when you talk to her you're struck by her lively mind and wry sense of humor.

Geneviève reads widely and speaks several languages, including the ancient and nearly extinct local one called Provençal. Her extensive knowledge of languages means that she can explain the meaning of any word or phrase you care to throw at her, plus she can usually cite its origin. As a teacher she's formal, rigorous, and what the French call *formidable.* In other words, she was just what we needed.

I was nervous about starting a weekly class of only Val and me. On the one hand, it would help me improve my French because I would get lots of attention from the professor. On the other hand, Val's been studying the language longer than me and all that attention would make abundantly clear how much better she is. But part of learning any language is accepting occasional (or in my case, frequent) humiliation so I've resigned myself to it.

The first time we had a class with Geneviève, she pulled a book off a shelf and asked us to each read a few paragraphs to test our pronunciation.

We failed.

I knew we were in trouble as soon as Val started. As she spoke, Geneviève began writing notes on a pad of paper. After a few sentences she started grinning. Then she started giggling. When it was my turn she put down her pen and started laughing out loud and wiping her eyes.

Geneviève is not one to mince words. "Your pronunciation is terrible," she said. Thus our first lesson went straight to the basics.

"You will begin by learning how to pronounce the letter R," she said. "You Americans pronounce this letter in the mouth."

"Well duh," I thought to myself, "of course we do. We talk with our mouths, don't we?"

But leave it to the French to be different. Geneviève explained that instead of the mouth, the French R comes from the back of the throat—kind of an "rrrr" sound that's a little like growling. She had us practice it over and over, growling louder and louder, until her dog got upset and started barking at us.

"Now I'll explain how to pronounce the letter U," said Geneviève. "It's very simple—when a U is in the middle of a word, you make a U sound. When it's at the end of a word, you don't make a U sound."

"Hm," I thought.

"Instead," she continued, "you make an 'O' shape with your lips at the same time you make an 'E' sound with your mouth."

You'd think the French would settle on just one vowel at a time, but no.

Next was the combination OU. Here we learned that again you use your throat—Geneviève described it as kind of like a dog howling. We had fun practicing that one until her dog joined in and the neighbors complained.

After the lesson I was talking to my English friend Joe about our class and he told me that many languages have their own unique way of pronouncing the letter R.

"For example," he said, "the English R is pronounced in the mouth like the American R but the sound is not the same. The difference is in the tongue." He then proceeded to explain how the English like to use their tongues.

"Joe," I replied, "we're friends and all but that is just WAY too much information."

In our next class I described this conversation to Geneviève and she launched into a long and very detailed explanation of how the *French* like to use their tongues. Let's just say that they're much more creative than the English.

Val and I practiced what we learned from Geneviève and eventually our pronunciation improved, but for a while we were very self-conscious, what with all our growling, howling and trying to make our tongues do strange new things.

After a few weeks of working on spoken French, Geneviève decided to test our writing.

"You will each write an essay," she said, handing us a thick document. "You'll read this article about the American government changing the rules on the aging of cheese, then you'll write a paper commenting on it."

This is where I was reminded how much better Val's French is than mine. And how much more she knows about cheese. She wrote a brilliant and incisive analysis of US cheese legislation going back to the 19th century. She compared French and American cheese making techniques, quoted famous figures in the history of cheese, and threw in a fondue recipe for good measure. I, on the other hand, was proud that I'd translated Monterey Jack correctly (*Jacques de Monterey*). You can guess who was going to be class valedictorian.

I've done my best to catch up to Val, though. One way is by reading *Le Monde*, France's leading newspaper. One day there was an article that used the term *tête-à-queue* and I liked the sound of it, so I looked it up and found that it means "reversing direction." It's an old term that comes from when cattle turned around, with their heads (*têtes*) ending up where their tails (*queues*) used to be. The article had used it to describe someone changing their negotiating position.

"Here's my chance!" I thought. "I'll use this in my next paper. Geneviève will be dazzled by my command of obscure French terms and give me an A+. Say goodbye to being class dunce!" So I used it to describe a TV cameraman turning his camera around 180 degrees.

I watched eagerly as Geneviève corrected our papers at the start of the next class. "Valedictorian, here I come!" I thought. She was partway through my paper when she got to the bit about the camera. She stopped correcting and looked at me sternly. Uh oh.

"No, no, no!" she said, "This is not at all correct. You can only use the term to describe COWS or perhaps sheep but *nothing else*." Then she put a big red mark over the offending words, one of many big red marks on my paper.

Usually I meekly accepted Geneviève's corrections but his time I wasn't ready to give up so easily.

"Wait," I said, "*tête-à-queue* was used in *Le Monde* to mean something else—look!" I had the article with me and showed it to her, which led to a lot of harrumphing. She was forced to admit that *Le Monde* was a pretty good citation.

One point for Keith!

Geneviève then walked over to a shelf and pulled out a thick book. "Let's consult the *Robert* dictionary," she said. She flipped through the book and found the definition, then pointed to it triumphantly. It was ambiguous but seemed to support her position.

Zut, one point for Geneviève. We were deadlocked. But two could play this game.

"Let's see how *Larrouse* defines it," I said, and pulled out my iPhone. *Larrouse* and *Robert* are competing French dictionary companies and I hoped they wouldn't see eye-to-eye on *tête-à-queue.* I opened up my online dictionary and found the definition. Like the *Robert,* it was ambiguous but seemed to support *my* position.

Now it was 2-1 Keith and I was feeling smug. I was going to the head of the class! But not so fast.

"There's a final arbiter," Geneviève announced. "The *Académie française.*" This is the august group that has the last word on any question relating to the French language. Its members are so revered they're called *Immortels.*

"I'll check their dictionary in the village library and report the results in our next class," said Geneviève. Then she leaned forward, looked me right in the eye and smiled confidently.

Let's just say that Val's class standing was not threatened for long.

French People Are Like Coconuts

"French people are like coconuts, Americans are like peaches."

I hear that a lot, but what does it mean?

The idea is that the French can seem aloof, or even rude. They're hard on the outside like a coconut, but when you finally crack that tough exterior you find that they're sweet inside. It's said that once a French person makes you their friend, you're a friend for life.

By contrast, it's said that we Americans are easy to get to know at first—soft and sweet on the outside like a peach. But beyond that delicious exterior is an inner core that's harder to penetrate. Some French only see the outer part of Americans and so they consider us "superficial."

As an American, I'm not crazy about being compared to a *fruit* and certainly not a peach. I'd rather be some cool kind of animal, like a panther or a wolverine ("or a sloth," adds Val helpfully). And I haven't found French people particularly hard to make friends with; you just have to make an effort. Take Sophie and Jacques.

We first met Sophie the year we lived in Le Thor and were looking for a "language partner" to help us improve our French. One of the hardest things about learning a new language is having the opportunity to speak it, especially when you are just starting out. Who wants to have a conversation with someone who is always searching for their words and making mistakes?

The answer is: someone in the same position. If you can find a French person who wants to practice speaking English and will let you practice speaking French, you both win. And if you are lucky like us, you become friends with your partners, so we were eager to find new ones.

We hadn't had any luck finding language partners in Le Thor until Val had the idea to ask at the tourist office. Happily, Sophie had been there the day before, looking for the same thing. The lady at the tourist office connected us and we started meeting twice a week over coffee. We liked Sophie and she must have liked us because a friendship was born.

After a few weeks of meeting at the local café, Sophie suggested that we meet the next time at her house. Partway through our language exchange, Jacques came home from running errands, decided we looked harmless and invited us to stay for a glass of champagne when we finished. Of course we said yes because who doesn't love champagne? After that they invited us to stay for lunch, then afternoon coffee, then chocolates, and our day together finally ended with a happy walk home late that afternoon. I guess we made it through Sophie and Jacques' coconut exteriors in record time.

That first lunch led to many more shared meals and drinks, bike rides, and trips to the movies, and once we even went on vacation together. We miss them when we're in California and consider them two of our best friends anywhere.

Maybe it was easy to get to know Sophie because she isn't actually French, she's Italian. She was born in Italy and moved to Paris as a child, so she speaks French with a Parisian accent and speaks Italian in the dialect of her native Calabria. She's petite and energetic and dresses like the chic *parisienne* she once was. Her homemade spaghetti sauce is legendary and she is renowned for her version of that delicious French mini-cake, *cannelé bordelais*. This is truly a woman who embodies two cultures.

Sophie once owned a restaurant near Disneyland Paris, back when it was first being built, and loves telling the story of how she introduced Disneyland's American staff to espresso.

"They would order coffee," she says, "and expect BIG cups because everything is BIG in America. But we Italians make the best coffee in the world and it's so good that just a few sips is enough. So I would bring a tray of espressos and set the dainty little cups in front of them."

"At first they thought I was joking, so they asked me where their coffee was. I explained that this was Italian coffee, *real* coffee, and it was all I served. They weren't happy because espresso is not only small but also much stronger than what they were used to. But they had no other choice so eventually they learned to appreciate it. By the time their work was over and they returned to the US, they were big fans."

"I have converted many Americans," Sophie notes with satisfaction.

Jacques, by contrast, is 100% French and proud of it. He was born in the apartment above the bar his parents owned and was a rebel as a youth. He once told me the story of the time he got drunk at a Spanish bullfight and decided he could do a better job than the matador, so he jumped the fence and ran right into the middle of the ring.

"What happened?" I asked.

"I took one look at that bull and ran out of there! He chased me and I somehow got away but I lost my glasses in the process. That was a scary drive home that night, with me still half drunk and squinting to see the road."

Jacques went straight from high school to the army where he began to get his act together. He succeeded so well that when Charles de Gaulle died, Jacques was part of the military honor guard at his funeral. What does he remember of that famous day? "We had to stand at attention outside the church for four hours...and it was hot as hell!"

After the army, Jacques earned an engineering degree and worked his way up to a senior position at one of France's largest companies. When offered early retirement, he jumped at the chance, trading in his suits and ties for t-shirts and shorts, growing a beard and letting his hair get long. I've seen photos from his corporate days and hardly recognize him, but he certainly looks happier today.

Jacques is a big, strong guy who enjoys working with his hands and in retirement has become a self-taught sculptor. His works in metal, wood and stone are scattered throughout the house and yard and sometimes when we drop by to say hello we find him banging away in his workshop. His hair and beard will be covered with wood shavings, or maybe bits of the rock that he's just chipped off a big slab.

They say that French social life revolves around the dinner table and it's certainly true for Val and me. We love to eat and sometimes I think of our life in France as a long series of meals with Sophie and Jacques—this one elaborate, that one a quick barbeque, and many of them picnics in the wild and beautiful Provençal countryside. We talk about everything, from the serious news of the day to *n'importe quoi* (politely translated as "whatever" and less politely as "the usual bullsh*t.") One of Sophie's favorite topics is American customs and how they differ from the French.

"Where do you shop for your food?" she once asked.

"At the grocery store, of course," answered Val.

"You mean just *one* store?" said Sophie, taken aback. "Don't you go to the outdoor market for fresh produce, to the *boulangerie* for bread, to the *boucherie* for meat, to the *fromagerie* for cheese, to the *patisserie* for dessert and to the *ferme* for fresh eggs? And what about wine? The wine you buy at a grocery store is…is…"

"*Merde,*" said Jacques.

"Yes, it's *merde! Oh la la,* the quality of food must be very bad in America."

Val tried to explain that many of the grocery stores in the US are actually quite good. But debating with a French person about food? Trust me, you're going to lose.

I have come to consider Jacques as my explainer-in-chief, helping me understand French culture. He reads several newspapers daily and his laid-back exterior masks a powerful intellect. I asked him once about *Le Monde* because I had noticed that its politics seemed to change. The first few years we were in France, *Le Monde* was very *gauche* and I considered it part of the Socialist camp. But then it switched and became conservative, espousing economic policies you might find in the pages of the *Financial Times*. What happened?

"It's simple," said Jacques. "*Le Monde* is THE newspaper in France, the one that all political leaders read. So it has a responsibility to counterbalance the current government and keep it from going too far. When there's a conservative government, it leans left. When there's a Socialist government, it leans right."

"So it changed because the conservative government of Sarkozy was replaced by the Socialist government of Hollande?" I asked, astonished.

"Exactly," said Jacques.

That's so different from the US, where the *New York Times* is always liberal and the *Wall Street Journal* is always conservative. To change your tilt because of the government in power—that's unique. And learning about *Le Monde's* shifting position is a small step toward my goal of understanding France.

Vive la France!

Val and I spend so much time in Provence that we're often asked when we are going to buy a place there. And I have to admit, the idea *is* romantic. We sometimes imagine having a cute little *maison* in St-Rémy, with a view of the Alpilles and a *boulangerie* around the corner. But then reality intrudes.

I always seem to be fixing something in our house in California—a faucet springs a leak or the microwave goes on the fritz. I have to keep the gutters clean and the trees cut back. And sometimes there are big jobs like resealing the driveway or replacing the water heater. It's no different from what any homeowner deals with, but when I think about having to do it for two houses that are thousands of miles apart, the romance of a home in Provence disappears.

Plus, Val and I don't want to be tied to a particular house. While we've settled on St-Rémy as the town to stay in, it's nice to be able to move around and try different places. And because we need a good-sized yard where our energetic dog can run, we usually find ourselves outside of town. Sometimes way outside, like our first place in St-Rémy.

It was quiet, beautiful...and almost impossible to find because it was on a dirt road that didn't even have a name. When we first went to check it out, we had to drive around for an hour before we found it. We passed one farmer four different times—he was trimming a tree and every time we went by he would look at us like he was thinking, "what are they doing way out here?" We even stopped a mailman, asking for directions, but he was as confused as we were. By dumb luck, we finally saw a tiny sign with the name of our place and an arrow showing us where to go.

The house was an old *mas*—a big Provençal farmhouse—built in the 1700s and beautifully cared for since. It had a huge yard, surrounded by a forest, and behind that you could see a single peak of the Alpilles. We came to think of that peak as our own personal Alpille.

The owner was an elderly lady we called Madame. She lived in a little apartment on the grounds, having moved out of the main house a few years earlier. The house still had many of her belongings, like the heavy, traditional furniture, lovingly cared for and passed down through the generations. Its dark wood had the kind of deep sheen that only comes from years of polishing. There were dishes galore, heavy plates with simple blue patterns on them, and a cabinet full of tablecloths made of fine linen. Copper pans hung around the stone fireplace. The place was spacious and serene, the nights silent except for the sound of trees creaking in the breeze.

And then there were the donkeys.

Madame loved donkeys. There were several that would show up from time to time, owned by neighbors so far away we couldn't even see them, and they would trot into our yard and scare the dickens out of the dog. We could hear them coming because they were always braying excitedly, hoping for a handout.

Madame, you see, collected stale bread for the donkeys from her favorite *boulangerie.* She would offer them baguettes, holding the long, skinny bread by one end while a donkey munched happily away on the other. *Crunch crunch crunch.* The donkeys were so well trained they would actually form a line and wait their turn. *Crunch crunch crunch.* After one had finished its baguette, Madame would shoo it off and feed the next.

This country home would have been perfect if not for the fact that it was so far outside of town. Our friends called it *le coin perdu* (the middle of nowhere) because they couldn't find it on their own. Any time they visited, we had to meet at the tourist office and guide them back to our place. So the next year we decided to stay closer to town.

We found the perfect spot just off the main road into St-Rémy. It was another old *mas*, with two-foot-thick stone walls and a vast yard in two parts, upper and lower. When the owner, Guillaume, bought the place his plan had been to build a second home in the upper yard, but when he started to dig the foundation he found Roman artifacts. It's forbidden to disturb such ancient remains so that was the end of the second home project, but it gave us an extra-large yard.

The property was right next to the Canal des Alpines, part of an irrigation system that feeds farms and vineyards throughout the region. Right outside our front gate was a waterfall where the canal's waters crashed down to irrigate fields below. We could hear its gentle roar at all hours and it helped to block out noise from the road.

The sunny kitchen was our favorite room, with its giant, arched windows that reached almost to the high ceiling. There was nothing we liked better than starting the day in the kitchen, eating breakfast and gazing out at our yard and the vineyards beyond, looking forward to another day in Provence. Outside our front door was a large stone terrace where we ate our meals when the weather was warm, and next to that was a gravelly driveway that made a perfect court for *pétanque*, the popular local game that's kind of like lawn bowling.

Guillaume stopped by once a week to take care of the property. He's a stocky guy with a thick Provençal accent and an ever-present smile, one of those people you like right away. Every time he came he would stop to talk, chatting about the weather and asking us if the plumbing was working properly (the house was centuries old, after all). And he always seemed to bring a gift—one time it might be strawberries, another time asparagus. And then there was the meat.

"Do you like ham?" he asked me one day.

"Sure," I said. "There's nothing better than a French ham sandwich."

"Then I'll bring you some ham from the butcher in Lamanon," he said. "He's the best in Provence and this ham will prove it!"

The next time I saw Guillaume he brought ham. And not just a slice or two, but nearly a pound—Guillaume doesn't do anything halfway.

"Did you like it?" he asked eagerly the next time I saw him.

"Yes," I replied, "it was delicious." I didn't have the heart to tell him we had only been able to eat about half of it.

"Then I'll bring you some sausages," he said. "They're even better than the ham!"

A week later Guillaume showed up carrying two bags loaded with more sausages than we could eat possibly eat. They were tasty but...gosh, that was a lot of sausage. Luckily our friends like sausage, so every time we visited one we would bring a few along as a gift. "Here," we'd say, "have some sausages!" It was a little odd but everyone appreciated them.

After the sausage it was muzzle salad. Guillaume wanted to be sure we tried it because it was the butcher's specialty.

"What's muzzle salad?" I asked. I like salads but hadn't heard of this one, and was curious what kind of salad a butcher would make.

"It's made from a muzzle, of course," said Guillaume, "a pig's muzzle. You know, its snout."

"Oh."

So muzzle salad it was, which wasn't as bad as it sounded, but we were glad when Guillaume went back to bringing us ham.

One day Guillaume invited us to his house for an aperitif. "Come by on Saturday at noon," he said. "Christine and the kids would love to see you." A midday *apéro* is usually just a glass of wine and some munchies, so we figured we would spend about an hour with Guillaume and his family and then be off. But we were wrong.

The first clue that this was not going to be a simple *apéro* was when we walked into the house and saw that it was full of people. Besides Guillaume and Christine and their kids, there was Christine's mother Marianne and her father Maurice, Guillaume's sister Janine, their friends Anne-Marie and Olivier, plus some kids from the neighborhood. I think word had gotten out that there were Americans coming over who sort of spoke French and everyone wanted to see this oddity, kind of like a three-headed cat. Or maybe they'd been watching old American movies and thought we would show up with cowboy hats and six shooters and do tricks with our lassoes.

The next clue that this was going to be more than a quick drink was when we saw the plates piled high with food, next to half a dozen bottles of wine and several homemade liqueurs. The grill was fired up and there were stacks of sausages at the ready. From the butcher in Lamanon, no doubt.

Val and I looked at each other. "I don't think we'll be leaving in a hour," she whispered.

The whole afternoon was very relaxed and friendly. There had been a commemoration of D-Day the week before so everyone thanked us as Americans for liberating France. We all raised our glasses as they toasted us with a chorus of "*Merci America!*"

I returned the favor by thanking them for French support in our war of independence, raising my glass with a hearty "*Vive la France!*"

Then they toasted us for our help in World War I. So I toasted them for the Statue of Liberty. Then they toasted us for jazz and I toasted them for Edith Piaf.

This went on for a while until I toasted them for French kissing and Val kicked me under the table.

My memories of the rest of the afternoon are fuzzy because all that wine kept my head buzzing for hours. But I certainly remember the laughter—these are people who have known each other for years and enjoy each other's company. And they could not have been more welcoming to us. It reminded me of the line from the movie *Casablanca*, "I think this is the beginning of a beautiful friendship."

And it was. Every year, we have lunches and dinners with the friends we made that day. Sometimes it's at our place, sometimes at Guillaume and Christine's, sometimes at Janine's. Or maybe we'll get together at Marianne and Maurice's place or the home of Anne-Marie and Olivier. They've welcomed us into their world and we're lucky to be able to share it with them.

Out Of Gas

Our American friends sometimes ask us, "How do you spend your time in France?" I think they imagine a trip to France being a vacation where all you do is run around and see the sights. And because Val and I visit every year they presume we're Super Tourists who see every sight imaginable. Or they think we've already seen everything and now we're bored and have nothing to do. But the truth is neither is true—we're just two people living in Provence and the business of living fills our days.

It should come as no surprise that eating and drinking take up a lot of our time—we're in France, after all. And you have to add to that the time it takes to prepare a meal. Shopping is not only a series of trips to specialized shops, it's also a discussion with each shopkeeper to decide what is *exactly right* for the meal you're preparing. And then the cooking takes time because food is serious business in France and you don't want to get it wrong.

We also spend a lot of time hiking and biking, which is necessary after all of our eating and drinking. Plus we occasionally go to a museum to see a new exhibition or to a movie theater to see the latest release. We have our weekly French class with Geneviève and we try to only read in French while we're in Provence—somehow it's easier to sit in a café and read a French book when everyone around you is speaking French. But we're slow readers in the language so that takes time. And sometimes friends from the US or Switzerland come and stay with us, so every year we spend a week or two hosting guests and showing them around.

Between guests and food and exercise and reading and living a French life, our days are full. And then once in a while something unexpected comes along that takes even more time. Like the day the country ran out of gasoline.

We had organized a trip to Switzerland and we would be driving there in a few days. We needed to fill up the car for the trip, so we went to our regular gas station on a Sunday. But when we got there we found a long line, which is very unusual for the weekend.

"What do you think's going on?" I asked Val. "Should I get in line?"

"You know how the credit card reader here sometimes decides to stop working?" she said. "It's probably that so let's come back tomorrow." I agreed and we headed home.

The next morning we were about to leave for our French class when my phone rang. I picked it up and it was Jacques.

"*Salut,*" he said. "I want to let you know that there's a big strike at the oil refineries and the country is running out of gas. Everyone is panic buying and the stations will be empty soon, so you should fill up your car right away."

I thanked Jacques for calling to warn us and then explained to Val what he had told me.

"That explains that long line at the gas station yesterday," she said, "but what do you think about filling up now? Do we want to be late to our class with Geneviève?"

We talked about it and decided that improving our French was a priority so we would wait and fill up on our way home from class. Strikes happen all the time in France, so how bad could this one be? We soon found out.

We finished our class and then went to our regular gas station, but to our dismay the entry was blocked with a big sign that said *VIDE* (Empty). Uh, oh.

"Let's try the station on the other side of town," said Val. "It's not on the main road so it doesn't get as many customers."

We drove there but again found a big sign that said *VIDE*. Now we started to get worried. We decided to try the next nearest station, a couple of miles away. When we got there we saw that it had a long line and figured that meant it still had gas.

"We should be ok," I told Val. "All we have to do is wait our turn."

Our car slowly crept forward and we were almost to the pump when we saw an attendant came out of the gas station. He was carrying a piece of paper and he walked up and down the line of cars, showing each of us what was written on it. It was bad news—he had scrawled *VIDE* in big letters. We had gotten to the station just a few minutes too late. I guess we should have listened to Jacques.

Now we started to panic. Val used her phone to hunt around online and try to find any news.

After a few minutes she found a message board that said there was still gas in a station twenty minutes away, so we raced over. We found a long line there, even longer than the last one, but people seemed to be filling up their cars. We got in line and, as we did, the sun broke through the clouds and started beating down on us. It quickly became uncomfortably hot.

"Should I turn on the air conditioner?" I asked Val.

"I don't know," she said, "maybe we should keep the engine off to save gas, just in case."

"You're right," I said. "Unfortunately." An hour went by, and then another, as we sat sweating in the car, slowly working our way to the pump. Around us we saw cars trying to cut in line while other cars honked at them and drivers shouted bad words at one another.

"*Quel bordel!*" I said, which made Val laugh. It means "what a mess" and we learned the expression from Sophie. Unfortunately she didn't tell us not to use it in polite company because *bordel* means not only "mess" but also "brothel." I learned this the first time I said it—loudly—and suddenly found myself facing a roomful of shocked expressions. Now it's kind of a private joke between Val and me.

After hours of waiting we finally made it to the pump. I grabbed the nozzle and it looked odd, somehow bigger than usual. "What's this?" I thought. I tried to put it in the opening to my gas tank but it wouldn't fit. What the heck?

"Let me try," said Val, who did an impressive job of trying to jam it in. "*Mince!* It doesn't fit—let me talk to the attendant." She got him to come over and he looked as hot and cranky as everyone else.

"It's because of your car," he said, "it's too new. This is an *old* station and it has *old*-fashioned nozzles that only work for *old* cars—that's why we still have gas left. Look around, do you see any other new cars here?"

I looked around and he was right. I hadn't noticed it before but we were surrounded by nothing but old bangers and grumpy drivers.

"Isn't there something we can do?" I asked, desperate now and feeling like a stupid American. "We've been waiting in line for hours!"

"No, sorry, that's the way it is. Now please move your car so the guy behind you can fill up." We got back into our car and drove off, frustrated and hot, and cranked the air conditioning up to high.

Val went back to her phone. After a few minutes she said, "I might have something—look at this."

She had found a map showing stations that still had gas. There were a couple of them in an out-of-the-way town we had never visited, so we rushed over and luckily their pumps were still working. The stations were rationing gas so we couldn't fill up, but between the two of them we got enough to make it to the Swiss border. What a relief.

This was our first experience with a serious French strike. While it worked out ok, it took almost an entire day to find the gas we needed—a hot, uncomfortable, nerve-racking day. Since then we've experienced other big strikes, like the one where we were stuck in a traffic jam miles and miles (and hours and hours) long. Strikes are something we've become used to, one of the few negatives to go along with the many positives of living in France.

And now when people ask how we fill our days in France, I just smile and say, "Oh, something always seems to come up."

A French Crime Spree

What began as a bike ride ended as a lesson in French auto insurance. I would have preferred just the ride.

One of our favorite routes begins out in the country, so we cram our bikes in the car and drive to the starting point. One day we parked on the side of the road, unloaded the bikes, and began our ride. Everything was fine until we got back and saw broken glass next to our car.

"That's funny," said Val, "I don't remember any glass there before."

"Look," I said, "someone broke our window. We've been robbed!"

Val said a very bad word and then, "I left my little black travel purse under the seat! How could I have been so stupid?"

We frantically checked the inside of the car. The thieves must have rifled through our belongings because everything was in disarray, with the glove compartment open and maps and papers all over the floor. Luckily, they had missed Val's purse and instead stolen our Styrofoam ice chest.

Real criminal masterminds, these.

The car, a rental, came with insurance so we found the insurance company's number and called them to report the broken window. They told us to file a report with the St-Rémy police department and when we got there, the officer manning the front desk turned out to be a real comedian.

"Our car has been broken into," said Val.

"Was anything stolen?" asked the officer.

"Nothing important, just an ice chest," said Val.

"They didn't get the sandwiches, did they?" he asked, looking alarmed.

"No," I replied, "we already ate them."

"Thank goodness!"

Then he took the car's paperwork and our IDs and started filling out a long form on his computer. While he was doing that, another officer came by "to investigate the crime scene." He was wearing a white lab coat plus a facemask, safety goggles, and latex gloves, and in one hand he carried a big box marked *Kit de Crime.* He left to inspect our car and came back a few minutes later.

"I have examined the crime scene," he announced dramatically, "and determined that your car's window has been broken."

Wow, I thought, these guys are *good!*

When the first officer finally finished with the long form, he printed it out, signed it and then loudly stamped it in a bunch of places. *Stamp stamp stamp stamp stamp.* The French just love to stamp paperwork and the more times the better. Val was about to sign the paper when I noticed an error—in the box for her marital status the officer had marked *Célibataire* (Single).

"Excuse me," I said, "but my wife is married. *To me.*"

"Oh, sorry! My mistake," said the officer.

"In fact," I continued, "we'll be celebrating our 25th wedding anniversary soon."

I noticed Val looking disgruntled. "Well," she said, "I was kind of looking forward to being single again. 25 years is a long time."

Ha ha, she's such a kidder! I think.

We finally finished the paperwork, shook hands all around and headed home. As we left, I remembered that we had been in this police station once before. Years earlier, when the car we were renting had been parked on a different country road, someone had broken into it and stolen a melon.

St-Rémy was definitely experiencing a crime wave.

The next step was getting the broken window fixed and then getting the insurance company to pay for it. This took much longer than expected. First, we called the 24-hour roadside assistance number that came with the car. They sent a repair guy to our house to patch up the car window temporarily, and after that we went to the auto shop to get a replacement window. This was on a Monday. They didn't have a replacement in stock so they ordered one and the shop manager told me that it would arrive on Wednesday at noon.

"Ok," I said, "can we schedule the work for that afternoon?"

"No, no," he replied, "there won't be time that day because we close at 4pm."

Ah yes, I thought, those famous long French working hours. "Ok, so how about the next day?" I asked.

"Of course not," he said, "we'll be closed for the holiday."

I'd forgotten that Thursday was a national holiday, one of *four* that month (this was in May). Those holidays put so many holes in the work calendar that the French call May the Swiss Cheese Month.

"No problem," I said, "how about Friday?"

"It is not possible!" he cried. "That's a bridge day and we'll be closed!" When a holiday falls on a Thursday, companies usually give Friday off to create a "bridge" to the weekend.

Geez, I thought, Wednesday is out, Thursday is out and Friday is out. I was getting exasperated but tried again. "Ok, fine, how about Saturday?"

The manager's eyes opened wide and he looked at me like I was crazy. "*Monsieur*, that is the weekend and of course we're closed. You don't expect us to work *all the time*, do you?"

We scheduled the work for the following Monday.

Once that was settled we began our long and painful discussions with the insurance company. Actually, "we" means "Val" because my French wasn't good enough for such a complicated subject. She had to make a lot of phone calls to the company and no matter what question she asked, like "Is there a deductible?" they gave her the wrong answer. For a while we were worried that we would have to pay a lot to have the car repaired but it finally turned out that everything was covered.

The insurance company also wanted paperwork—lots and lots of it. AND they didn't follow up on their commitments. AND one person never seemed to know what another person had done. It was very frustrating. In other words, we felt right at home! It turns out that insurance companies are the same everywhere.

On the promised Monday morning, we took our car in for repair. But when we returned to pick it up, the paperwork that the insurance company was supposed to send to the repair shop *still* hadn't arrived. So Val and the manager called the company together and talked to them for a while. Well, "talk" is a polite description of what they did. Let's just say that I learned some new bad words. Eventually everything was sorted out (and more papers were stamped and hands were shaken) and we were able to take our car home.

We hoped this was the end of the crime spree.

I Wish I Were A Dog

If there's really such a thing as reincarnation, I want to come back as a dog. In France.

Val and I love dogs and our first one, Rodin, moved with us to Switzerland. We were surprised by how dogs there could go anywhere, like into restaurants. I still remember the first time we saw one, lying under a table at the feet of its owners. Suddenly it stood up and bumped into a passing waiter...who promptly apologized!

France is as dog-friendly as Switzerland and when we began our part-time life in Provence, we of course brought along our new dog Lucca—Rodin having gone to doggie heaven by then. But after a full and happy life, Lucca passed away just weeks before we went to Provence one year. That was a sad springtime.

When we got back home to California we went back to the shelter where we had adopted Rodin and Lucca and this time found a cute little gal we named Mica. We call her that because her fur is black and shiny like mica, the volcanic glass, and as an added bonus it's the same word in both French and English. Only the pronunciation is different, so when she's in America she's "my-ka" and in France she's "me-ka."

Mica loves Provence. She's not crazy about the long flight over and neither are we, but within a few minutes of arrival we've all forgotten about the trip and we're ready to explore. The hassle is worth it because in France a dog can go practically anywhere. We don't have to leave Mica at home when we go out, we just bring her along.

French people adore dogs and we always receive good service when she comes along with us to a restaurant. She's sometimes even served before we are! "Would you like me to bring a bowl of water?" the waiters and waitresses will ask. "And can I pet your dog?" More that one waiter has told us that dogs are better behaved than a lot of diners.

All our friends like Mica so when they invite us over they invite her, too. Jacques is especially taken by her and is always cooing "*ma belle*" (my beauty) and offering to keep her when we go back to California. I keep an eye on Mica when we're getting ready to leave Provence because I'm afraid he might try to kidnap her.

We see dogs everywhere in Provence—wagging their tails in stores, sniffing along on hiking trails, splashing around in the local lake. I once saw one zipping down the street in a motorcycle sidecar. Its owner was riding the bike and the dog was sitting next to him in the little car, happy as can be with its ears flapping in the wind.

French people come up to us all the time, wanting to pet Mica. We'll start to chat and they're always surprised when they find out we're Americans because what American would have their dog with them in Provence? We like to think that they've mistaken us for locals and that makes us feel more French, but it's really just thanks to Mica.

Mica gets a lot of attention from other dogs as well. She's super friendly and wants to say hi to everyone, and when we come across another dog there's always a festival of tail wagging. Her special pal is Sophie's dog Ugo, who's getting up in years but who becomes downright frisky whenever this cute young babe shows up. I think she's good for his health.

When we go somewhere with Sophie and Jacques, the dogs always come along. They love picnics because they can run around and sniff to their heart's content while we have our lunch. And if we're having a lazy dinner at a café, they lie in wait under the table, hoping some food falls off of a plate so they can scarf it up.

For me, one of the best parts of having Mica is when we go to a winery and Val and Sophie get bored while Jacques and I taste wine. Off they'll go to walk the dogs, strolling through the vineyards and (probably) complaining about their husbands. The good news is that it leaves Jacques and me without anyone to monitor our buying, which is why our wine cellars are always well stocked. Thank you, *ma belle!*

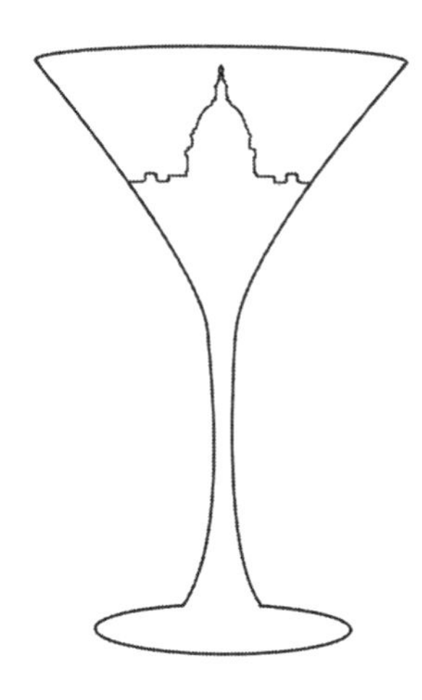

Sex And Politics

I'm kind of a political junkie. I'm not crazy about actual politicians but their antics are always entertaining. I follow French politics by reading the paper and watching the news on TV. It gives me something to talk about with my French friends, plus I've learned that politics are even more entertaining in France than back home.

One day I was reading the paper and a headline about a "sexy politician" caught my eye. "Well, those are two words you don't see together very often," I thought. I read the article and found out that there had been a poll asking French women,

"What politician would you like to have a summer fling with?"

"They would never have a poll like that back home," I thought. "It's way too sexist." And if they *did* conduct such a poll, American women would take one look at our politicians, think about a fling with them and immediately flee the country (probably to France).

I showed the article to Val. "Honey," I asked sweetly, "if I were a politician and they did this poll, would you vote for me?"

She looked me up and down and said, "Don't quit your day job."

Later I read another article and found out about the "oldest politician" rule. France is broken up into a bunch of regions and each one has a legislative council. These each elect a president and the party with the most seats in the council wins, but once in a while there's a tie.

It seems that one of the regions up north had deadlocked and no party had a majority. When that happens in the US—a tied election of some kind—there's always a simple way to pick the winner. Some places flip a coin, others have the candidates draw straws, and I think in Las Vegas they pull from a deck of cards and the high card wins. But it's not that way in France.

The article said that the conservative party had won the council presidency because it had... the *oldest* counselor. It turns out that *that's* the tiebreaker—not the best counselor, not the most experienced, but the oldest. If that rule had existed back in Biblical times, the Canaanite Party would have dominated elections because they had ol' Methuselah on their side.

But it's TV that really lets me see French politics in action. One year, early in the election season, there were about a dozen candidates still in the running for president. France likes to give everyone equal time so they organized a big debate at 8 o'clock one evening.

I wanted to see this so I made sure to finish dinner early and plopped myself down in front of the TV. I flipped to Channel 2 and saw all the candidates milling around in the center of an amphitheater, almost like they were in the bottom of a pit.

When it was time for each candidate to speak, the camera would zoom in on him or her. You'd see the candidate and the people in the front row behind them, but their seats were slighted elevated so you couldn't see their heads. The people in the audience all wore dark clothing that kind of blended into the background, making only their hands stand out. This meant that the

TV screen was filled with the candidate's head and, behind it, what appeared to be disembodied hands. It was kind of spooky.

The fun started when the conservative party candidate made his opening statement. After he had spoken for a minute or two, I saw a pair of hands behind him begin to twitch.

"We must forge tighter bonds among our citizens..."

One hand, floating to the left of the candidate's head, started to scratch the other one. And scratch. And scratch. *And scratch.*

"France must protect its people from the scourge of terrorism..."

Scratch scratch scratch

It was mesmerizing. I couldn't look away.

"Now is the moment for a new spirit in our country..."

Scratch scratch scratch scratch scratch

I turned Val, "Can't we call a dermatologist for this poor guy?"

The candidate finally finished but I don't remember what he said. Apparently nobody else did, either, because he plummeted in the polls the next day. Maybe the moderator should have passed around some Jergen's Lotion.

But the funniest political stuff I've ever seen on TV was the time there was an election to the European Parliament. Every country in the European Union was electing deputies who would do...well, nobody knew quite what because no one pays attention to the European Parliament except to complain about it.

In France, it doesn't take much to field a slate of candidates, so there were 48 (yes, 48) different parties running. And some had very interesting names.

New Anti-Capitalist Party
Union of Struggle Against the Banks
For a Royal France at the Heart of Europe
Cannabis Without Borders
Esperanto, a Fair Common Language for All
Libertarian Program for a Europe Setting an Example Against Sexism and Precariousness

As with the presidential election, every party received equal airtime to run TV ads. A few were shown every night and they were one of the highlights of the day. Well, except for the ads for the major parties. Those guys actually had a chance of winning so they played it safe and had dull ads, all about responsibility and balancing the budget and blah blah blah. No wonder nobody liked them.

Then there were the ads for the various Green parties, which were all rainbows and lollipops—

"We believe in a clean environment, good jobs for everyone, and puppies."

And there was something called the Regionalism Party. Their ad was an angry guy who kept shaking his fist and railing against the *Jacobins* in Paris.

"Do you know who the *Jacobins* are?" I asked Val. "A bunch of guys named Jacob?"

But she didn't know so I looked it up. It turns out that they were a group that existed way back during the French Revolution, so getting upset about *Jacobins* was like complaining that you just can't find a good snuffbox these days.

But then the New Deal Party ad came on, my all-time favorite. It would never be allowed in the US.

The ad starts with a naked young couple lying in bed and energetically doing, um, what naked young couples do. Suddenly a lady charges into the room and sits on the bed.

"You're trying to make a baby, aren't you?" she demands.

"Uh, yes."

"Well, have you thought about what kind of future that baby is going to have? Have you thought about whether your baby will have political leaders who will make sure there are good jobs, fair wages, and a clean environment?"

"No," says the guy, looking miffed, "I definitely was *not* thinking about *that* just now."

"Why yes," says the gal, "I was!"

"So vote New Deal in the European elections!" says the lady.

I can't wait for the next election.

The Court Of Love

Sometimes when Val and I are walking around Provence, it feels like being in the middle of a French History theme park, with attractions like *Romanland!* and *It's a Medieval World!* We can't go a hundred yards without bumping into something old, sometimes ancient.

It starts with prehistory—just north of us are the world's oldest cave paintings in the *Grotte Chauvet*. How old are they? Let's just say they were painted back when Team Homo Sapiens was still duking it out with Team Neanderthal for mastery of Europe (spoiler alert: we win).

The real cave is too fragile for tourism and so the French government built a perfect replica, like the famous one at Lascaux. A guided tour takes visitors through the dimly lit cave to see vivid paintings of horses, lions and rhinos. There are bear skulls scattered around the floor because it was once used by hibernating bears. Early humans would move in at the end of winter after the bears left.

Can you imagine being the guy who had to make sure the coast was clear? "Go ahead, Gork, check and see if the bears are gone. And if you don't come back, can I have your club?"

Then there are all the reminders of the Roman Empire, like the famous *Pont du Gard* aqueduct, as tall as a sixteen-story building. Throughout Provence are Roman triumphal arches and ancient bridges and old grain mills. And the Roman arenas in Arles and Nîmes are still in use, holding events that draw thousands of spectators.

I remember once attending a concert in the Arles arena and thinking, "People have been using this place for over 2,000 years—those Romans were incredible engineers." We have talented engineers today, too, but do you think that we'll still be using iPhones thousands of years from now?

Besides all the artifacts from the Roman era, there are plenty from the Middle Ages as well. After the Roman Empire collapsed, social order did too and marauding bands of soldiers and thieves roamed the countryside. The people of Provence ran for the hills—literally—building the *villages perchés* (perched villages) that tourists adore today.

Provence has scads of medieval abbeys and churches and the strong Catholic presence is understandable. After all, one of the first kings of France, Clovis I, converted to Christianity way back in the 5th century. What I find surprising is that there are deep Jewish roots as well.

During the Middle Ages, Jews were persecuted throughout France but found refuge in Avignon and the adjacent papal territory called the *Comtat Venaissin*. Known as *les Juifs du Pape* (the Pope's Jews), they lived under his protection and formed the core of Jewish life in France for centuries. They were crammed into tiny ghettos and forced to build upward due to the lack of space—you can still see one of their medieval "skyscrapers," five stories tall, in the town of L'Isle-sur-la-Sorgue.

Of all the historic remains in Provence, my favorite is Château Romanin, not for what you can see today but for the story behind it. Built by a Templar knight, it was not only a fortress but also an important Court of Love, where noble ladies presided over "questions of gallantry."

Questions of gallantry? Does that mean you could you be prosecuted for using the wrong fork? I've tried to imagine how this court worked—perhaps a damsel would press charges against a knight for a violation of protocol. A court would convene, attended by all the nobles of the region, and the proceedings would begin. It would go something like this.

Noble Lady Prosecutor: "We hereby charge Sir Goeffroi with Failure of Gallantry in the First Degree."

There are murmurs in the court—this is a very serious charge.

"Given his obvious lack of manhood, we demand public humiliation! Sir Goeffroi must be forced to wear tights and a wig for 90 days."

Gasps are heard. The knight's wife faints.

Noble Lady Judge: "Order, order in the court!" She flutters her hankie to calm the crowd.

Chivalric Public Defender: "If it please the court, I wish to make reference to His Royal Highness the King."

All heads are bowed at the mention of the royal name.

"I would remind the court that our mighty King himself likes to...ahem...wear tights and a wig. It's all the rage at the Palace of Versailles. It looks downright unmanly if you ask me but he's the King so there you go. I respectfully ask the court to consider another punishment for Sir Goeffroi."

Noble Lady Judge: "Ah, well, you're right. It wouldn't do to mock our noble King."

She thinks for a moment.

"Off with his head, then."

This sort of thing might explain the French obsession with following social rules *very carefully.*

Going To The Butcher

One of the things Val and I enjoy the most about Provence is the food. We go in the springtime when the fresh fruits and vegetables start appearing—first the strawberries and asparagus at the end of March, then the cherries, then the peaches and apricots and on and on. It's like every week when we go to the market there's a nice surprise waiting for us.

And then there's the meat. In St-Rémy we buy many of the same things we do in California, like chicken and lamb, but in Provence it's usually from small producers whose animals live in the countryside rather than on factory farms. And we buy other things that are hard to find back home, like rabbit and bull. It's all tasty, even the meat we buy at the giant *hypermarchés*, but the best comes from the small, traditional butchers.

These butchers are masters of their profession and often come from a long line of butchers, the latest to uphold a family tradition. *Boucheries* are an essential part of any Provençal village and an important civic institution—if you want to eat well, get to know your local butcher.

The first time we stayed in St-Rémy, in *le coin perdu*, Madame introduced us to her favorite butcher. She's known him for decades and put in a good word for us. It's good to have connections.

But there's one thing to know about a village butcher shop, and it's that you can't be in a rush. Everyone gets personal attention and takes as long as they want, which can sometimes be a long time. Val and I might walk into our butcher shop and find, say, two customers ahead of us. She'll turn to me and say, "Ok, this will take about 45 minutes."

The shop is run by a husband and wife who take great pride in their work. When you order a piece of meat, the butcher asks how you'll prepare it. He cuts off any extra fat, trims around the bone, and cuts it into the size you want. If you want hamburger, he takes a piece of beef, runs it through his grinder, and forms it for you while you wait. Patty by patty. And he offers homemade goodies like *paté*, salami, *ratatouille*, stuffed vegetables and at least four kinds of sausage. The butcher's wife dishes out these prepared items and runs the cash register while the butcher handles all the cutting.

If you are a local, the butcher and his wife will take the time to chat with you. How's the family? How are your bunions? How will you prepare the stew? For how many people?

And then there's the salt discussion.

"Do you salt your food?" the butcher will ask.

"Yes, but not too much," the customer will reply.

"My doctor tells me to use less salt," the butcher will say. "It's because of my age, you know. But I don't listen to him."

"Oh, you're just like my husband," the customer will say. "He puts too much salt on his food."

The butcher's wife will chime in, "*All* husbands put too much salt on their food!"

Once we came in to buy a couple of slices of *paté en croute* (*paté* in a pastry) but the customer before us had just bought some. The butcher's wife decided that the remaining log was too small to cut us two nice pieces, so she went to the back room to find a new one. That took a while. Then we decided to order a few other things and that took a while longer. Finally it was our turn to pay, but the customer after us was a very old woman and the butcher had just finished serving her. Of course we let the old lady pay first so she didn't have to stand too long.

"Please go ahead, Madame," Val said.

"*Merci*," the old lady replied. "Now where did I put my wallet..."

She fished around in her purse for a while and finally found her wallet. Then she slowly counted out the exact amount, coin by coin, and all we could do was wait patiently. When the old lady finally finished, we were ready to pay but then the phone rang—someone wanted to place an order for Sunday.

This led to a long discussion between the person on the phone and the butcher and his wife. How many people did she need to feed? What seasonings would she use? Should she pick it up at 11:00? No, maybe 12:00. No, 11:00 would be better. Finally they settled on 11:30.

And you wonder why it takes 45 minutes.

Another time we went to get a *gigot d'agneau* (leg of lamb) for a big dinner we were hosting. We were the only ones in the butcher shop this time, so there was no wait and Val explained what she wanted.

"For how many people?" the butcher asked.

"Ten," said Val.

"Ah, the *gigot* in my case isn't large enough for your dinner," said the butcher. "I'll cut you a new one."

So off he went to the back room and came back carrying not just a larger leg of lamb, but the actual *back half* of a lamb. Oh my, we don't see this sort of thing in California! At least the wool had been removed. The butcher turned on his electric saw and in two minutes flat the lamb was cut in half, feet removed, trimmed of excess fat, deboned, and tied with a string. Then came the cooking discussion.

"How will you prepare the lamb, Madame?" the butcher asked. Val explained her marinade and roasting plan.

"That will be excellent, but I must advise you of one important thing," said the butcher. He looked at Val gravely. "Under no circumstances should you use a temperature higher than 180 degrees!"

Val wondered how the *gigot* would cook properly at a measly 180 until she remembered that temperatures in France are in Celsius.

"And do you want the bones I removed?" continued the butcher.

Val wasn't sure, so why not ask the expert? "What do you recommend?" she asked.

"Ah," replied the butcher, "the bones will make a nice *jus* for the meat. Place them next to the lamb, cover them with olive oil and butter, add a full head of garlic plus salt and *herbes de Provence*."

What better advice than from a butcher? Val followed his instructions and now has the recipe for a delicious sauce. She served it to our French friends and they enthusiastically gave her the seal of Provençal cooking approval.

As much as we like our butcher and his wife, they're getting up in years and we know they'll retire soon. It's unlikely anyone will replace them because their kids have gone off to other careers and don't want to take over the family business. It's like that with a lot of these small shops, especially the butchers and bakers. The work is hard, you're on your feet all day, and the pay isn't much.

Young people have other opportunities and they often follow a different path. It's hard to blame them—I'd probably do the same in their shoes—but it's sad to see the old ways fading away. There are fewer and fewer of these traditional butcher shops, replaced by sleeker and more efficient versions. They're part of a vanishing world that we're lucky to enjoy while it lasts.

You Couldn't Make This Up

The year Val and I lived in Le Thor and met Sophie and Jacques, we also met Marie-France and Xavier. They were our next-door neighbors in the converted monastery where we all lived, one that had housed generations of Benedictine monks before being sold to developers. We became friends with Marie-France and Xavier over dinners and *apéros* on our terrace or theirs, and then we introduced them to Sophie and Jacques. It turns out that the four of them have a lot in common so they became friends with each other as well. We still laugh about the fact that it took a couple of Americans for them to meet each other.

Marie-France used to run a clothing company, importing shirts and fabrics from India. She had gone there to live in the 1960s, back in her hippie days, and figured out how to make a living as an importer. Later she became an antique dealer with a shop in L'Isle-sur-la-Sorgue, a town with the largest antiques market in France, which is where she met Xavier. She's retired now but you can still see a bit of the old hippie in her, from her casual-chic style, to her inquisitive mind, to her ability to find beauty in even the smallest things.

Xavier, like Marie-France, is a retired antique dealer. Their house is full of exotic objects from around the world, like Burmese alms bowls and Ethiopian wedding necklaces, so visiting them is like going to a museum. Xavier is now a photographer, traveling with Marie-France to countries like Libya and Vietnam and taking stunning photos that he shows at local exhibitions. He has a full, grey beard and the air of an explorer—it's easy to imagine him in some rugged country, snapping away under the blazing sun.

But there's something surprising about Xavier—he's a car nut. An *American* car nut, no less. He stays up till the wee hours to watch NASCAR races on TV and once even made a special trip to see the Daytona racetrack in Florida. He doesn't race competitively but a few times a year he and his buddies leave their wives behind to go bomb around the Sahara Desert in 4x4s.

I've come to think of Marie-France and Xavier as two of our cultural guides. They know that Val and I are trying to learn more about France and Provence and so they go out of their way to introduce us to things we might not come across otherwise. For example, one time at their house, Marie-France told us we were going to have *poutargue*. It didn't sound very good when she described it—a bunch of fish eggs squished together into a lump, dried, cured in sea salt, and then coated in wax.

When Marie-France brought out the *poutargue,* it was a fluorescent orange color and the shape of a hockey puck—not appetizing at all.

"People eat that?" I asked.

"Oh yes," said Marie-France, "it's very traditional. In the old days, the fishermen of Marseille would eat *poutargue* with bread and butter for breakfast. And wine, of course." She was born in Marseille and is an authority on local culture.

Marie-France cut up the hockey puck and then brought out some bread, spread butter on it and put a few bright orange slices on top.

"Try it," she said. It wasn't a suggestion.

I didn't want to eat it but you don't mess with Marie-France, so I timidly took a bite. And it was tasty! The salty *poutargue* and the creamy butter went really well together. It was a reminder to always try new things, even if you aren't sure about them at first. After all, wasn't that one of the reasons we were in France?

Another time, Xavier decided that we should be introduced to French *avant-garde* theater, so he and Marie-France took us to a local performance. It was put on by a private group, the kind that foreigners like us rarely hear about, and I felt like we were being admitted into a secret club. But I should have known that the show would be rather strange when I read the description.

Emergence. *It is the story of the urgent need to share, the story of resistance and hope in the face of fear. We surround the authors, and indeed others, to hear how to think with words in the face of evil.*

In other words, *The Lion King* it was not.

The performance space was in an underground artist's studio, filled with artwork that can only be described as weird—stuffed birds that looked like they were still in their death throes, sculptures of demented-looking bats, and vases of creepy black flowers.

"What have we gotten ourselves into?" I said to Val.

"Sorry, what did you say?" asked Xavier, who I didn't realize was standing right behind me.

"Oh hi, Xavier," I said, thinking fast. "I was just...ah...telling Val how interesting the artwork is."

In the middle of the room was a big table with a white tablecloth, two burning candles, a basket full of bread, and pieces of paper scattered here and there. Three performers sat on one side of the table, posing like Jesus and the disciples at the Last Supper.

The central character was a man wearing a big white scarf and a paper crown, the kind you get at Burger King. To his left was a woman in a fur coat and to his right was one in a wedding dress, complete with veil. All three sat very still, as if frozen in place. There were chairs surrounding the table for the audience to sit in.

I looked around to make sure Xavier couldn't hear me and whispered to Val, "Doesn't this seem strange?"

"It's artistic," she whispered back. "We're in France, remember?"

After a while the owner of the studio banged on the wall and told everyone to take a seat. Val and I sat opposite the actors and while we waited, loud rock music started playing on a repeating loop, over and over again, but the actors still didn't move.

Finally the lights dimmed, the music stopped, and the actors began eating bread. Then they randomly picked up papers from the table and read from them. They were passages from books or poems, I couldn't tell which, because it was a kind of florid language that I had a hard time following. And to be fair, part of my problem was that the actors were talking with their mouths full.

"Can you tell what they're saying?" I whispered to Val.

"Shhh!" she said. "This is good."

After a while the actors stopped reading, cranked up some new music and started dancing madly around the room, jumping up and down and flailing their arms—I had to duck once to avoid being hit by a flying elbow.

I leaned over to Val and said, "Good thing this isn't one of those audience participation shows."

After a few minutes of this the music stopped and the actors, now out of breath, went back to reading. They opened bottles of wine and passed glasses of it to the audience, but before we could finish they collected the glasses back and emptied whatever was still in them onto the tablecloth. Then they dumped out the wine in the bottles. The tablecloth became soaking wet, wine dripping onto the floor—I had to move my chair back because it was splashing on my shoes.

The grand finale started with the lady in the fur coat crumbling up a paper and eating it, chewing slowly. Mr. Burger King burned the other papers, one by one, holding each one up for us to see. Meanwhile, the lady in the wedding dress stroked a ceramic cow skull that had a ceramic carrot sticking through it, while munching contemplatively on an actual carrot herself. And then the lights went out and the show was over.

It was so ridiculous that I thought, "You couldn't make this up."

The lights came back on and the audience applauded wildly, leaping to their feet and shouting "*Bravo!*" and "*Magnifique!*" I applauded politely but was thinking, Whaaaaaat?

I turned to Val. "Did you understand that?"

"Well, it was certainly artistic," she said, and kept applauding.

After that we all went outside to where a table had been set up with drinks and snacks. I sipped a glass of wine and listened while people discussed the show—one guy kept talking about "Rimbaud" and "Baudelaire" while others nodded knowingly. I felt like I was in a group of French intellectuals and should be wearing a black turtleneck and beret, smoking a hand-rolled cigarette. But I still had no idea what the guy was talking about.

If this was part of my French education, I'd just flunked the midterm.

Books That Change Your Life

My setback with *avant-garde* theater made me realize that I lacked knowledge of deep French culture. There had been references and allusions that others had understood but which went right over my head. I needed a better grounding in the basics, and especially literature, so I resolved to read only French books when I was in France. I imagined this would make me all erudite and able to say things like, "Well you know, old sport, Racine is *much* wittier in French."

I decided to start with what I knew, so I read more books by Marcel Pagnol, my favorite French author. Pagnol lived nearby and wrote about

Provence so his books helped me understand the local people and customs. Then I added in some Jules Verne and a bestseller from the local bookstore.

This went so well that I got cocky and decided to tackle Molière. That was ambitious because he's *Monsieur Big* and French is sometimes called "the language of Molière." I figured that if I could understand one of his books it would practically qualify me for French citizenship. I chose *L'école des femmes* (The School for Wives) because it was less than 100 pages long—how hard could that be?

Um, hard. Really, really hard.

The book is thousands of rhyming couplets written in archaic French. Me reading it was like a French person with a modest command of English who decides to tackle *Hamlet*. I was a fool to even try.

Well, I may be a fool but I'm a stubborn one and once I start something I want to finish it. So I worked my way through the book, a few pages a day, and finished it in about a month. I'm sure there's a lot I didn't understand, and it gave my dictionary a good workout, but I have to admit that it *was* funny. Though I'm not planning to put *Molière's Greatest Hits* on my birthday wish list anytime soon.

After this, I realized that my study of French literature was hit or miss, a book here and a book there, but what I needed was more of an overview. Then I heard about a TV special called "The 20 Books That Have Changed Your Life" and it sounded like exactly what I was looking for. It was the result of a nationwide poll and the winning books were counted down like on an old Top 40 radio program. I found a recording of the show online and settled in front of my computer to watch it.

A panel of distinguished writers was on hand to provide commentary and the host started by asking what books had changed *their* lives. Several of them mentioned *Letters to a Young Poet* by Rainer Rilke, which I had never heard of but which sounded like the sort of book a distinguished writer would cite. Then one of the panelists brought the conversation to a sudden halt.

"The Bible," he said, "especially the Gospel of Saint John."

In the United States it would be completely normal for someone to cite the Bible, but here in secular France it was downright shocking. The panelists were visibly uncomfortable and looked down at their shoes, not knowing what to say. There was an awkward silence before the host finally mumbled a few words and moved on. It was a reminder of how deeply different France can be from the US.

Then the countdown began, starting with the last five books.

20 – *Les Misérables*, Victor Hugo
19 – *Madame Bovary*, Gustave Flaubert
18 – *The Diary of Anne Frank*, Anne Frank
17 – *Perfume: The Story of a Murderer*, Patrick Süskind
16 – *The Lord of the Rings*, J.R.R. Tolkien

These books got a lot of love from the panelists. How could they not? Hugo! Flaubert! We're talking about some of the all-time greats! Now all I have to do is read them. Darn.

15 – *Crime and Punishment*, Fiodor Dostoyevski
14 – *The World According to Garp*, John Irving
13 – 1984, George Orwell
12 – *Harry Potter*, J.K. Rowling
11 – *La Peste (The Plague)*, Albert Camus

You could almost see the thought balloons over the panelists' heads: "Camus together with... GARP? And HARRY POTTER? *Sacré bleu*, what has this country come to?" They were so upset that they didn't say much, except for the one who muttered, "Well, Harry Potter certainly sold a lot."

Then it was on to the Top Ten.

10 – *Les Fleurs du mal (The Flowers of Evil)*, Charles Baudelaire
9 – *One Hundred Years of Solitude*, Gabriel Garcia Márquez
8 – *Her Lover*, Albert Cohen
7 – *The Alchemist*, Paul Coelho
6 – *Le Grand Meaulnes (The Lost Estate)*, Alain Fournier

Márquez was lavished with praise and one panelist called his book, "the most important epic tale of the 20th century." I was happy to hear that because I've actually read it, but then I realized he wasn't French so I'm sure if it counts.

The final five were revealed one at a time, with drum rolls and dramatic music.

5 – *À la recherche du temps perdu (In Search of Lost Time)*, Marcel Proust

But of course. You can't have a list like this without those famous *madeleines*. But I wonder, has anyone ever actually read all *seven* volumes of Proust's masterwork? I think *non*.

4 – *L'Écume des jours (Froth on the Daydream)*, Boris Vian

Seriously, who translated the title into English? *Froth on the Daydream*? That sounds gross—no way I'd read it.

3 – *Voyage au bout de la nuit (Journey to the End of the Night)*, Louis-Ferdinand Céline

Very dark, very bitter. Kind of like French coffee.

2 – *L'Étranger (The Stranger)*, Albert Camus

I felt sorry for poor Camus. He had two books on the list, one about a plague and one about a stranger—not exactly uplifting subjects. Why was he so bummed out?

Finally, the countdown reached the big Number One, the most influential book of all. I wondered what it could be, maybe a masterpiece by de Beauvoir? Or Sartre? I, of course, was rooting for my pal Molière.

But no. Instead it was a beautiful little book that just about everyone has read.

1 – *Le Petit Prince (The Little Prince)*, Antoine de Saint-Exupéry

All the panelists loved this. As one said, "It asks questions about life that other books try to answer."

The host then told the history of *Le Petit Prince*. In 1942, Saint-Exupéry was depressed and having trouble writing. All he could do was doodle. His agent noticed that he kept drawing cartoons of a little boy, over and over. Exasperated, the agent suggested that Saint-Exupéry write the story of the little boy, thinking it might pull him out of his funk. The rest is history.

And I've read it! Adding in some of the other books I've read, like Garp (shh), I thought that maybe I was ready for another shot of *avant-garde* theater.

Then I remembered the cow skull with the carrot and thought, mmm, no need to rush into things.

Learning The Rules

Over the years, I've had to see various French doctors for one thing or another. And I'm always struck by how cheap medical care is in France. Office visits are about $30 and X-rays are $25. And that's not just the co-pay, it's the entire amount! The quality of health care is about the same in France as it is in the US, yet the costs are vastly lower. Why it's like that is a mystery to me.

Another thing that strikes me is how people act in waiting rooms. In a doctor's office back home, I'll check in with the receptionist and then sit and wait until my name is called. Maybe I'll look at a magazine or fiddle with my phone, but rarely do I talk to the other people in the waiting room.

The French, by contrast, have what I call the Official Waiting Room Protocol. Everyone knows it and, like other social rules in France, it's serious and it's complicated and you'd darned well better follow it.

What is the Protocol, you ask?

When someone enters a waiting room, they must say hello to the people already there. There's no slinking in and taking a seat—no, no, that wouldn't be polite! Instead you have to say the magic words and *you've got to get them right.*

The easiest thing is to say *Bonjour* as you enter, but that's too easy and so it's frowned upon. Instead, you are expected to tailor your greeting to those people already in the room.

This means that if there's only one man there, you say *Bonjour monsieur.* For multiple men it's *Bonjour messieurs.* To an individual woman you say *Bonjour madame* and for several women you say *Bonjour mesdames.* For a room with both women and men you are required to use the complicated multiple-person-dual-gender *Bonjour messieurs-dames.* Getting your greeting wrong means you have probably insulted somebody, like implying that a man is a woman or the other way around. Do this and you'll be sure to get a dirty look.

To properly follow the Protocol, you need to do a quick scan as you enter a waiting room and calculate both the number *and* gender of its occupants so you'll know what to say. Normally that's easy but it can be tricky if there's a guy with especially long hair or maybe a fellow who's carrying a man purse. And don't get me started on tattoos and body piercings.

You'd think that saying hello to everyone would be the end of it, but no, this is France. Next is the responding—not only do *you* greet everyone as you enter but *they* greet *you* in return. This means that every time you say *Bonjour madame* or *Bonjour messieurs-dames* or whatever, you receive back a chorus of *Bonjours*. But not just plain old *Bonjour*—no, the Protocol demands that the gender rules still apply.

Should the people in the waiting room say *Bonjour monsieur* to you? Or is it *Bonjour madame*? Again, the decision should be easy, but what if *you're* the dude with the long hair and the man purse and all the tattoos and body piercings? Suddenly, everyone in a crowded waiting room has to make a split-second decision, and it's vitally important that each and every one gets it right. Which, of course, never happens.

In other words: chaos!

Pharmacies have their own sets of rules. Like the US, France has over-the-counter drugs that don't require a prescription. But unlike the US you can't just take what you want. Instead, you have to wait in line to see a pharmacist, and then describe your problem so that he or she can dole out the appropriate medication.

This wouldn't be a big deal except that French pharmacies are usually small, which means that everyone in line can hear what you're saying. And I always seem to get the pharmacist who's hard of hearing and can't understand my French, so he keeps asking me, in a loud voice, to repeat myself. This means that a visit to the pharmacist goes something like this.

Me: "I need some medicine for a mumble mumblemumble on my mumblemumblemumble."

Pharmacist: "Speak up! You say you have a HORRIBLE LOOKING FUNGUS on your WHAT?"

The surprising thing is that the people in line are never fazed by what they hear, I guess because they've been going to French pharmacies all their lives. I might be standing in line and hear personal revelations that shock me, while everyone else looks kind of bored. Unless the subject is Vaseline.

Ah, Vaseline. I've used it for years because I have very dry skin on my elbows that occasionally cracks and bleeds. Regular hand lotion doesn't fix it but Vaseline does the trick so I always have some around. For me, having a jar of Vaseline in the medicine cabinet is about as unusual as having a bottle of ketchup in the refrigerator.

Not so in France. No, in France Vaseline seems to be used for one thing and one thing only: as a sex aid. And you can only get it at a pharmacy. So when you ask the pharmacist for a jar of Vaseline, everybody in the pharmacy—and I mean everybody, including the pharmacist—perks up.

Me: "May I have a jar of Vaseline, please?"

The people in line start to point at me and whisper.

Pharmacist: "You want WHAT? You need some VASELINE? Hee hee hee."

The people in line elbow each other and snicker.

I hate French pharmacies.

Another thing that's unusual about the French medical system is physical therapy, which I needed the year I broke my wrist. I've been to physical therapy in the US and it's always in some sterile building with scary looking equipment. The therapist will put me on a machine with lots of buttons and flashing lights and a name like *BodyTech KineMax 4200*. Then she'll give me a smartphone app that beeps when I forget to do my home exercises and I can never figure out how to turn the darned thing off.

By contrast, my French therapist's office was in a building hundreds of years old, with thick stone walls and ancient equipment. My favorite gadget was the one for strengthening my wrist: it was nothing more than a series of old doorknobs nailed to a board. I turned them left and right, left and right, starting with a small doorknob and gradually progressing to larger ones—the last was so big it looked like it came from a castle or something. The equipment might have been low tech but it got the job done and was much easier to use than that *BodyTech* thingy.

My therapist was outgoing and friendly and he didn't speak a word of English, so every week was a little language lesson. And he was funny. When I told him about my bike accident and how a kamikaze squirrel had attacked me, he looked very serious and told me to watch out for French squirrels.

"Maybe," he said, "the bad squirrel in America told his friends here to finish the job."

Wine And Friendship

Val and I didn't know much about wine when we moved to Switzerland—in California we might open a bottle for a special occasion but that was it. Then we found ourselves living in a Swiss village that had been making wine for over 1,000 years.

Wine was part of daily life there, a glass or two at dinner, and our neighbor Alexandre became our mentor. He kept his wine in a nuclear bomb shelter under his house (the Swiss all have one—it's required by law) and used to joke that, "If the big war ever starts, at least I'll die a happy man." Alexandre introduced us to wines from all over

Europe and gradually they became part of our lives.

Now we live several months a year in France, where wine is an important part of the culture, and I want to learn as much about it as I can. Wine is also a big part of my relationship with Jacques and together we spend a lot of time with wine—buying it, talking about it, swapping favorite bottles, and of course drinking it. In France, to say that a meal is *bien arrosé* (well watered) means that the wine is flowing. Our meals together are definitely *bien arrosé.*

Jacques and I are always on the hunt for new wineries, ones with good, inexpensive wine. One of our favorites is about an hour north in Gigondas and we make a special trip there every year to stock up our cellars. Unlike the fancy wineries I'm used to in California's famous Napa Valley, this one looks like a farm because, well, that's what it is. It's nothing more than a couple of buildings in the middle of a vineyard, with tractors and pickup trucks in the driveway. The tasting room is not much bigger than a walk-in closet, with plain white walls and a bar at one end. Like a lot of French wineries, this one has been in the family for generations and is run by two cousins and their wives.

We usually do our tasting with Mathieu, the winemaker, or Bernadette, his cousin's wife. Mathieu looks exactly as you'd expect—a farmer-winemaker with calloused hands, a firm handshake, and dirt on his boots. His wines aren't famous but they have a sterling reputation in Gigondas itself.

"Every year we have a competition in the village," he told us one time. "It's only for the winemakers, about a hundred of us, and we all want to win. My wine always finishes in the top ten." He stood up straighter. "This year I was third!"

We've become regular customers and that has its advantages. One year the vintage was so good that Jacques and I quickly drank every bottle we had (ok, Sophie and Val helped). The next year when we did our tasting we tried to buy some more of that excellent vintage but Bernadette told us that alas, it was finished.

Jacques wasn't so sure. Maybe they had a secret stash?

"You *really* don't have any?" he asked. "Maybe just a few bottles in the back?"

"Oh, no," said Bernadette. "Sorry, it's all finished."

But as our tasting progressed, from whites to rosés to reds, Jacques kept asking about that wine.

"Well," Bernadette finally admitted, "we do have a few bottles that we've saved for special customers."

"Why Bernadette," said Jacques, flirting shamelessly, "those wines are almost as beautiful as you! Aren't we special enough to have a few?"

Ah, the French and the art of seduction. We left with six bottles each.

Another favorite winery is in Estézargues, a village not far from the *Pont du Gard* aqueduct. All the winemakers in town share a big production facility, so while the winery in Gigondas looks like a farm, the one in Estézargues looks like a factory. The building is big and square and when you walk into it you see boxes stacked everywhere. You have to be careful that a forklift driver on his way to the shipping dock doesn't run you over.

Near the front door is a small office with a tasting bar attached. The ladies working in the office do the tastings and they enjoy taking a break from paperwork, so our tastings are always long and relaxed. We go there so often that Jacques and I have *cartes de fidélité* (frequent buyer cards) that give us special discounts.

Our tastings usually start with all four of us—Jacques, Sophie, Val and me—but eventually Sophie and Val get bored and go outside to walk the dogs.

"Let's go, Val," Sophie will say. "Ugo has to go *pipi*."

"I'm with you," Val will say, yawning. "Mica and I could both stand to stretch our legs."

This leaves the menfolk without adult supervision. One time when they did this I looked at Jacques and said, "You know what this means, right?"

"Yes," he said, "we get to buy more wine!"

One of the best parts about going to Estézargues is the picnic we have after our tasting, next to an abandoned church a few miles away. It's on a hill that gives us beautiful views in all directions—we see vineyards, olive trees, rolling hills, and a few buildings scattered here and there. It looks like nothing has changed since forever.

The church is centuries old and always seems very peaceful. But then one day when we pulled up for our picnic, we saw the front door open and heard banging inside. How odd, we thought, what's going on in there?

Sophie, never a shy one, charged right in to find out.

"*Coucou!*" she called out. "Anyone here?"

Inside was an old guy repairing a wall. We could see that it had been crumbling, its stones falling to the floor, and he was reinforcing them one by one. He explained that he was part of a local group that was refurbishing the church.

"We started with the roof," he said, "and then continued with the floor. Now we're working on the walls. We don't receive any money from the government, we're just a group of volunteers trying to preserve our local heritage." He had a folder and showed us some before-and-after photos. The group did beautiful work and the church looked much better than it used to.

The man had been working on the church for years and was happy to talk about it. Too happy, in fact. He talked for so long that I wasn't sure we would ever start our picnic. We had brought some ripe, smelly cheeses and their aromas were wafting out of Sophie's picnic basket next to me, making me hungry. Sophie and Val felt the same way I did, so every few minutes Sophie would say, "Thank you, Monsieur, this has been very interesting!" and the three of us would edge towards the door.

Unfortunately, Jacques was fascinated. He likes to work with his hands and wanted to know every detail, so each time Sophie would try to get us out of there, Jacques would make like Detective Columbo and say, "I have just *one more* question." Monsieur was always happy to oblige.

Finally, the three of us gave Jacques the stink eye and he reluctantly stopped asking questions. We went outside, to the little lawn beside the church, where we spread out our blanket and Sophie and Val unpacked lunch—olives, salami, cheese, some cherries, a couple of baguettes. It was a perfect picnic lunch, topped off by a bottle (or maybe two) of the wine we had just bought. We ate and drank while the dogs snoozed in the sun.

Whenever we share a meal with Sophie and Jacques, whether it's a simple picnic or something more elegant, the wine we share is usually a modest one. It's nothing that will impress the wine experts but it doesn't matter—we love it. We love the taste, we love the smell, we love the fun of buying it together and we especially love the pleasure of drinking it with these friends we cherish.

In France they say that the best wine, the very best, is a wine that you share with friends. It doesn't matter what kind of grapes are in it, or the vintage, or the name on the label. It's the act of drinking it with friends that makes it great.

That lesson was one of the most important of my entire French education.

I Will Never Speak Good Français

Val and I continue our French lessons with Geneviève every year, and the good news is we're always making progress. The bad news is we're always finding new errors to make. Sometimes it feels like we're hamsters in a big wheel, running hard but going nowhere.

Learning French is like one of those home repair projects that turn out to be much bigger than you expect. All you plan to do is put a new washer in that kitchen faucet that's dripping, and then you start the job and find that the faucet itself needs replacing, but that model isn't available anymore so you buy another one, but then the new faucet requires a special connection to the water pipe. The next thing you know the sink is all torn up and there's a plumber and a carpenter working in your kitchen and your wife keeps asking when they'll be finished. It's like that with French—just when you think you have your arms around it, you discover more and more things you need to learn.

In our class, Geneviève periodically has us translate articles from English into French. One day I had to translate the word "aggressive" and so I chose *agressif*, which seemed obvious to me. But when I turned my paper in to Geneviève it wasn't quite so obvious to her.

"Oh, no," she said, "that won't do at all."

It seems that some annoying little *nuance* meant I'd picked the wrong word yet again. We hear *nuance* a lot. Geneviève has high standards and wants to make sure we learn French EXACTLY the right way. As she puts it, "It's important to express your thoughts precisely." In this way she's like a lot of French people who are proud of their beautiful language and want it to be spoken properly. I've seen French people on the street correct each other for what seem like teeny weeny language mistakes, something I never see back home.

In the US, we're more relaxed about *nuance* and precision. English has become a world language and many people learn it after their own native tongue. This means that lots of English-speakers have accents and limited vocabularies but are still able to get their point across—a factory in Germany can order parts from a supplier in Brazil and then ship the finished product to Vietnam, with everyone communicating in "pretty good" English. That sort of thing is fine with me, which is why *agressif* seemed perfectly acceptable, even if it maybe wasn't precisely the right word. But it wasn't acceptable to Geneviève.

"In French," she explained, "*agressif* is a very strong word that implies physical violence. But here you are describing two people who are only talking in an unpleasant way and you need to translate the word differently."

So now I had to play our game of Find A Word That Geneviève Will Accept, a game I play a lot. What word could I use that had the right *nuance*?

"*Froid?*" (unfeeling)

"*Non.*"

"*Sec?*" (harsh)

"*Non.*"

"*Méchant?*" (nasty)

"*Non.*"

This went for a while as I ran through all the French adjectives I could think of, plus a few I made up. Finally I cajoled Geneviève into accepting *acerbe* (acerbic) but I could tell she wasn't happy with it. I think she only agreed because she'd gotten a cramp in her mouth from saying *Non* over and over.

Another time we worked on tenses. French has a ridiculous 26 different ones, which is 23 too many for me—I'd be happy just learning a simple past, present and future. But Val loves all these tenses and so does Geneviève. I still remember the time the two of them had an animated discussion about the miniscule differences between *imparfait,* which I kind of understand, and *conditionnel passé premiére forme,* whatever that is. Learning French with these two sometimes feels like a math class where one minute we are doing addition and subtraction and then suddenly they zoom off into quantum theory and leave me far behind.

We spent several classes just on the *subjonctif* tense. This is a hard one because there's no equivalent in English; it's a kind of moody tense you use "to convey a sense of doubt." It's a subtle thing that they probably use in all those French movies I never understand.

It seems like a stupid tense to me but I decided that, dang it, I'm going to figure it out. I told myself I would study and study and then measure my progress. I found a test online that would let me see how I was doing—it gave me 24 sentences and all I had to do was choose between answer A (*subjonctif* tense) and answer B (a different tense). I could take the quiz over and over with new sentences every time.

"This is perfect," I told Val. "There are only two choices so even someone who doesn't know a word of French can flip a coin and get 12 right."

"I see," said Val, which wasn't very encouraging. Then I took the test and got 12 right and she tried not to laugh.

So I studied harder, asked Geneviève lots of questions the next week in class, and then took a new quiz.

I got 13.

In our next class, I explained my dismal results and showed Geneviève the quiz.

"These sentences are terrible," she said. "They look like they were written by an American." That buoyed my spirits—the questions must be the reason I was doing so badly.

"But," she continued, "you still should get at least 20."

Sheesh.

So I searched around some more and finally found a website with a good explanation of the "sense of doubt" business. It said that when you are less than 70% sure of something, you should use the *subjonctif* tense. I was amazed because it means that every French person is doing advanced probabilistic calculations in their head at the same time they carry on a conversation. Is something 56% certain? 83%? French people know! I can only shake my head at their impressive mental powers.

But while this may be easy for French people, it's too hard for me. I've decided to eliminate the darned tense from my vocabulary, along with this whole sense of doubt nonsense. Instead, I'll always be really, really certain about everything. I'll act like I'm absolutely sure of something whether I know what I'm talking about or not. If I can master this kind of empty confidence and be annoyingly certain even when I have no idea what I'm talking about, I might have a bright future in politics.

Exploding Soup

Our first long stay in Provence was in a small town called Mollèges, not far from St-Rémy. We became friends with the owner of our rental house, Pascal, who grew up in the area and never left because why should he? He appreciates the simple pleasures in life and Provence has them in abundance.

Pascal is one of those people I admire because he's so...what's the word? Centered? Grounded? You feel calmer just being around him. I remember the time we were having dinner on his terrace and he said, "Look at us—we're enjoying good food, good wine and friendship. We're in the most beautiful place on earth. If we want, we can go for a hike in the Alpilles tomorrow, or a bike ride, or maybe go fishing in the lake. Do we need more than this?"

Another time he gave Val and me a tour of his garden, stopping to explain every flower and encouraging us to taste every herb. The tour took over an hour because, as Pascal told us, we needed to take our time to appreciate "the gifts of the land."

We could use more of this attitude in Silicon Valley, where so many people hunger for that next promotion, or that new car, or that trip to an exotic destination. I try to adopt Pascal's attitude as much as I can, but it's easier to do when I'm in Provence.

French people love to talk about food and Pascal, a chef, is no exception. One time we had him over for dinner and he talked about fish for the entire evening. Nothing but fish. You'd think this would get boring fast but it didn't, maybe because Pascal was so enthusiastic. We sat spellbound as he gave us a whole discourse on fish cleaning, fish preparation, fish storage. How you should put a few dabs of vinegar on a fish before freezing it. How some types of *rouget* should be fried and others baked. How you can tell if a fish smells bad because it's supposed to (there are some stinky varieties) or because it's spoiled.

As he was leaving that evening, Pascal said, "I've talked about fish enough and now I'll show you! Come over next week and I'll make you *bouillabaisse*."

Wait...homemade *bouillabaisse*? We were honored because it's a local specialty and a rare treat that takes all day to prepare. We couldn't wait.

When the big day arrived and we walked into his house, Pascal had a big pot of soup simmering on the stove. He poured us each a glass of wine, put out a bowl of olives, and sat us down in front of his kitchen counter.

"Let's start with a history lesson," he said. "Legend has it that *bouillabaisse* was invented long ago by the fishermen of Marseille. They didn't want to eat the high-class fish they caught because those fetched the best prices, so they created this dish from the rockfish no one wanted."

"To make *bouillabaisse*," he continued, "you start with the soup." He was referring to the fish soup called, logically enough, "fish soup" (*soupe de poisson*).

"I'm using six kinds of rockfish because that's what was fresh in the market this morning.

They're bony and ugly but delicious if you know how to cook them." I looked down at one, the famously ugly *rascasse,* and saw what he meant. "I always make sure to include *saint-pierre,*" he added. "The fish is named for Saint Peter and you can see a spot on its side—in Provence we say it's the thumbprint of the great fisherman himself."

"You season the fish with saffron and other spices, then cook them with onion, fennel, garlic and tomato," Pascal continued, "and don't forget the white wine—that's very important!" He explained that this mixture is then ground up, bones and all, into the thick and richly flavored *soupe.*

"And you have to grind it by hand. *Never* use a blender."

"Why not?" I asked.

"Because if you spin a bunch of hot liquid around at high speed, the pressure builds up and it will EXPLODE. I know from experience." He pointed to his white kitchen walls, where we could see faint saffron-colored stains here and there.

As Pascal spoke, he sometimes referred to a yellowed cookbook titled *La Cuisinière Provençale,* the bible of local cooking. "I always use this," he said, "to respect our traditions." He must use it a lot because I could see that some pages had fallen out and been taped back in.

Next to the stove was a platter of fish marinating in olive oil and saffron, ready to be cooked. Pascal turned up the gas burner and waited until the *soupe* came to a boil, then put the fish in and turned down the flame. He leaned forward conspiratorially. "I've just shown you the big secret to making *bouillabaisse,*" he said. "You have to lower the temperature at precisely the right moment or the fish will be overcooked."

"It's also where the name comes from," he continued. "You bring the soup to a boil (*bouiller),* then lower (*baisser*) the temperature. Put *bouiller* and *baisser* together and you get *bouillabaisse.*"

A few minutes later everything was ready and we sat down to eat. Pascal had laid out a basket of small round toasts and a dish of *rouille* that he had made, a kind of saffron mayonnaise with lots of garlic. We spread *rouille* on the toasts and dropped them into our bowls of *soupe*, making little floating islands of deliciousness.

"Not like the frozen junk they reheat in restaurants and tell you is the real thing, eh?" asked Pascal with a sly wink.

Then we had the fish with boiled potatoes and more *soupe* sprinkled on top. I can't remember if I had seconds or maybe it was thirds but I do remember that it was the food of the gods. We finished our meal with strawberries from the local market and I was so full I wasn't sure I'd be able to eat the next day.

As the evening ended and we said our goodbyes, Pascal told us, "Everyone loves *bouillabaisse* and so do I, but I don't think of it as just a dish. No, for me it's a lesson in our history as a Mediterranean people. If we pay attention, *bouillabaisse* can teach us about the diversity of our fish and about our spices and about so much more. Every time I make it, it's a great moment for me to be able to share it with family and good friends."

A great moment, indeed.

Picnics In Provence

One of the ways that Val and I enjoy in the beauty of Provence is by going on picnics, usually simple affairs that we combine with a hike or sometimes a bike ride. The Alpilles are full of winding trails and there's nothing better than exploring them with Mica—we'll head off in a direction that looks promising and always be rewarded with stunning views.

One favorite spot, especially on a hot day, is Peiroou Lake outside of St-Rémy. It's hidden in the mountains so you have to know where to go, but finding it is worth the hunt. The lake is actually a reservoir, created by the Romans thousands of years ago, with sheer rocky walls along one side. There's a patch of grass at the end, shaded by a grove of pine trees, where we sit and have our picnic. Mica likes to go in the water to splash around and sometimes we join her.

A few miles north of St-Rémy is Avignon, sitting majestically along the banks of the Rhône River. The city is full of wonderful views but I think the best one is actually outside of town, on Barthelasse Island. It's in the middle of the river and has a long, grassy esplanade that faces Avignon. From there you can look across to the city's medieval ramparts and, above them, see the golden angel atop the pope's old palace, glistening in the sun. Sometimes we explore the island and then have a picnic on the esplanade, gazing at the city and watching boats slowly cruise by.

As much as we enjoy our picnics, just the two of us, they're even better when they're with Sophie and Jacques. Sometimes they're simple but often they're elaborate and that's part of the fun. They usually start with a phone call.

"*Coucou*," Sophie will say, "we have to get together. I haven't seen you in so long!" This usually means it's been about a week.

"Yes!" Val will say. "The weather is nice so how about a picnic?" Sophie will agree and the planning will begin.

"I can bring a salad," Val will say.

"What kind?" Sophie will ask.

"Some kind of green salad," Val will say. "I'll see what I have."

"That will be nice," Sophie will say, thinking about what will complement a green salad. "I'll make a rice salad."

After a bit more discussion, Val and Sophie will agree on a few dishes and then each will bring whatever she wants to fill out the menu—hors d'oeuvres, olives, charcuterie, that sort of thing. And of course they'll decide who's in charge of the cheese, because no picnic is complete without some choice morsels. Meanwhile, Jacques and I do the important work of deciding what wines to drink.

A full-on picnic with Jacques and Sophie is quite the event. Sophie will spread a colorful blanket on the ground, then open up her picnic basket and bring out the plates, glasses, silverware, and real cloth napkins. She and Val will unpack the food and Jacques and I will open the wine, usually a bottle of white to go with olives and nuts for our *apéro*, while the dogs run around.

Next will come the main courses of things like salami and ham, sometimes a quiche or a tart, some salads, and plenty of bread. Then the cheese course and, after that, the desserts. We wash it all down with red wine, or maybe rosé if it's hot, and finish with chocolates. Later we'll find a café and wake ourselves up with cups of strong French coffee.

We like exploring Provence together, discovering new picnic spots. One of our favorites is in the Cedar Forest above Bonnieux. To be above Bonnieux is quite a statement because it's a high hilltop village that looks down on the Luberon Valley. But the Cedar Forest is higher still, and we picnic in a shady spot that looks out over the entire valley floor, a patchwork of small farms in different colors—bright green vineyards, darker green olive groves, brilliant yellow patches of rapeseed, and purple lavender fields. We sit and enjoy the view and our food and wine, then take a quick snooze before making our way down the steep, winding road home.

Our most memorable picnic was thanks to Bernadette, at our favorite winery in Gigondas. We had gone there on our usual wine buying expedition, tasting with Mathieu and learning all about the latest vintage. We usually go on a picnic after our tasting, in a vineyard below the beautiful village of Séguret, but this year it was too windy for that and we weren't sure where to go. We asked Bernadette for a recommendation and were surprised when she crooked a finger and said, "Follow me."

She led us out behind the winery and pointed to an old stone table on the edge of the vineyard. "How about this?" she asked. "The building protects it from the wind and the view is very nice."

We all looked at each other and I could tell we were thinking, "This is perfect but there's just one problem..." There were no chairs and it didn't make sense to sit on the ground and not take advantage of the table. It was embarrassing to mention this because we didn't want to look a gift horse in the mouth.

Finally Jacques spoke up. "This is beautiful Bernadette! We'd love to picnic here but unfortunately we didn't bring any chairs."

"No problem," said Bernadette, who then hurried off. She came back a few minutes later, this lady who must be in her 60s, lugging four heavy folding chairs. "*Voila!*"

We all thanked her and Sophie tried to return the favor. "You are so kind, Bernadette," she said. "Will join us for lunch? We would be very pleased if you did."

"Thanks," Bernadette said, "but I can't. My husband is coming in from the vineyard and we always have lunch together. But could I join you afterwards for coffee?"

There was another embarrassed pause, and now it was my turn to speak up. "Bernadette, we'd like to do that," I said, "except we don't, uh, we don't have any, er..."

"Coffee?" asked Bernadette, grinning.

"Um, right, we don't have any coffee," I finally got out.

"I expected as much," she said. "Don't worry, I'll bring it with me." And with that she headed off for lunch with her husband. We all looked at each other, amazed by her generosity.

Comfy in our chairs and with the beautiful vineyard in front of us, we spread out our picnic lunch on the stone table and enjoyed it with one of the bottles we had bought at the winery. Then Jacques and I finished off a second bottle while Sophie and Val took the dogs for a walk. A couple of hours had gone by when we saw Bernadette walking towards us, carrying a tray with five cups, a big pot of coffee and a plate of cookies.

"I made the cookies myself," she said shyly. "They're biscotti because I know Sophie was born in Italy. I hope you like them."

"I'm sure they're delicious!" said Sophie, and of course they were.

"I'll be right back," said Bernadette, and disappeared for a moment. She returned carrying a chair for herself and a bottle of wine for us.

"Remember that vintage you liked so much?" she asked, looking at Jacques. "Last year you convinced me to sell you some that we'd saved for special customers. We finally ran out but I found a bottle in my personal cellar and I brought it for you."

"Oh, Bernadette, that's so generous of you!" said Jacques, as he jumped up to give her a kiss on each cheek. It's one of the things French people do when they receive a gift. The rest of us stood up and kissed Bernadette as well. I'm not sure but I think she might have blushed.

We spent the next couple of hours together, with Bernadette telling us about her life. "I grew up in Violès," she said, "a small village a few kilometers away. I met my husband Jules when I was young and we got married shortly after and moved here. Looking back now, I realize that I was only just a girl! But it was the custom then that people married young."

"Jules and I live in a small house next to the winery, which is where we raised our family. Now our kids are grown and it's just the two of us. Our oldest son Sébastian lives nearby and works with Jules in the vineyards. He'll take over the business someday. Virginie and I—that's Mathieu's wife—we do all the winery's paperwork. It's a quiet life but it suits me. I'm a country girl and I can't imagine living in a big city. I need to see the vineyards and breath the fresh air."

She went on to tell us more about her life and ask us about our own. She seemed to enjoy our conversation, maybe because it was something outside her usual day-to-day. We enjoyed the conversation as well and were struck, once again, by what a kind and gentle soul she is. It was getting late when we finally said our goodbyes, all of us looking forward to the next time we would see each other.

I wouldn't say we're close friends with Bernadette but we're more than acquaintances. There's a special connection we share because we all love Provence, and wine, and the simple pleasures of life. Sharing those things together, as we sat around that stone table beside the vineyard, made for one of the best picnics Val and I have ever had.

My Favorite Cheese

Shirtless men splashing in a pool. A guy wearing a gigantic horse's head. A fellow dancing with a gorilla.

Yes, it's time for Eurovision!

Eurovision is a cross between *The Voice* and the Olympics, a big singing competition where each European country nominates an act to represent it. Fans go crazy waving flags, painting their faces, and screaming. It's one of the highlights of my Provence stay every year.

Eurovision started back in the 1950s and the most famous winner is ABBA, who rocked Eurovision with *Waterloo* in 1974 and went on to worldwide fame. Other performers haven't achieved nearly the same success; in fact, most sink without a trace. But on the night they win they're the biggest thing in Europe.

Hundreds of millions of people tune in to the finals, making it the most-watched program of the year, but try as I might I have yet to meet one of them. Every year, I ask all my French friends, "Want to come over and watch Eurovision with me?"

"No, no!" they say, looking vaguely alarmed. "I don't watch that. Maybe my *grand-mère* does but no, not me."

Riiiiight. Let's just say that Eurovision draws such a huge audience that there must be a lot of grandmothers in France. *A lot.*

Maybe Eurovision is a guilty pleasure, something you enjoy but are afraid to admit to, like comic books or disco music. Personally, I think people are afraid to say they like it because of the cheese. Wait, you ask, don't the French love cheese? Well yes, but not this kind. Eurovision acts are legendary for being cheesy and that's my favorite part. I can listen to good music any time, but cheesy? That's a dying art.

I fell in love with Eurovision the first time I saw it. I still remember the singer in a slinky dress belting out her number while a burly guy behind her ran inside a giant hamster wheel. Why? Who knows! It was so ridiculous I was mesmerized.

Every year, I can't wait for the finals, marking my calendar and blocking out the evening. And I especially look forward to the act from Azerbaijan because it can always be counted on for something wacky. I'm sure Azerbaijan is a fine country with a sophisticated culture, but they've figured out that what wins votes at Eurovision is cheesiness.

One year the Azerbaijani group performed in front of what looked like a dark, creepy forest. One guy sang while a couple of others writhed around on the ground in front of him.

"Why don't those guys have shirts on?" I asked Val. "And are they really wearing...studded dog collars? With leashes attached?"

"Yup," she said, "and check out those pants! It looks like they have on leotards with diapers underneath."

Serious cheesiness!

Azerbaijan lightened things up the next year, with hunky, bare-chested singers prancing around in football pants and sparkly gold shoulder pads. Val liked the act a lot, and not for the music.

Then there are the scary acts.

One year Austria was represented by a 70s-style band, complete with bad 70s rocker haircuts, kind of like big shag rugs on their heads. They weren't scary until their piano burst into flame—on purpose—and firemen had to rush onstage to put it out.

Scarier still was the Georgian singer dressed like a warrior goddess from the land of the undead. She wore all black—high leather boots, crow feathers sticking out of her shoulders, and a kind of dark tiara of death. She was scary, but in a we're-just-kidding-here kind of way.

Then there was the band from Cyprus—they really were scary. The lead singer looked like he might have escaped from prison, with tattoos all over his shaved head. The rest of the band was locked inside a giant steel cage, which was probably for the best.

Most countries sing in English, which is nice because I can understand their lyrics, but one always sticks to its native tongue. Now who might that be? Yes, the ever proud French. Unfortunately, the judges don't appreciate this linguistic patriotism and put France near the bottom every year.

Politics showed up once, in a funny way. Political songs are banned from Eurovision but Ukraine found a way to sneak one in. It was right after Russia had invaded Ukraine and annexed the part of the country called Crimea.

The Ukrainian singer's song was about the brutal expulsion of her ancestors in 1944. Where were they expelled from? You guessed it, *Crimea*. And who did the expelling? Yes, *Russia*. So every time the singer got to the line about "and my grandmother suffered," she would turn and glare at the Russian singer sitting in the audience. We all got the point.

Eurovision may not add much to my understanding of France, but it's part of my life in the country, a bit of low culture to balance the high culture of Molière and *avant-garde* theater. Watching it makes me feel like an insider, participating in a noble and longstanding European tradition. And it sure is fun—there's nothing like a dancing gorilla to brighten your day.

The Real French National Sport

Jacques and I were watching TV one afternoon, the famous *Tour de France* bike race. We were drinking wine and eating snacks as the cyclists pedaled their way up a mountain, cheered by thousands of spectators lining the road.

All those French people cheering and waving flags made me think of a question. "Would you say that cycling is the French national sport?" I asked. Jacques is an avid sports fan and I wondered what he thought.

Jacques pondered the question for a moment. "Certainly it's a contender," he said. "It's very popular here and France has won more Olympic cycling medals than anyone else." He paused and took a sip of wine. "But soccer is even more popular than cycling so I would say that's our national sport."

"Oh, c'mon!" I protested. "Soccer is popular everywhere. The French national sport should be something more French. What do you think—maybe *pétanque*?"

Jacques laughed. "That's certainly French," he said, "and very popular here in Provence. But can it be a real sport if you drink pastis while you're playing?"

We both laughed and thought about that as we watched the bikers continue their climb. Then I had an idea and grinned.

"I've got it!" I said. "It's a sport that's very French, it's very popular, and the French are the best in the world."

Jacques saw my grin and wasn't sure he was going to like my idea. "And that would be...?" he asked tentatively.

"Street demonstrations!" I cried. "Think about it. The storming of the Bastille! The Paris Commune! And didn't the student riots in 1968 almost bring down the government?"

"Ah yes," said Jacques, suddenly quiet. "May '68. I was there, you know."

"No way!" I said. May '68 is a landmark event in French history, a political earthquake whose aftershocks are still felt. I was thrilled to learn that someone I know had actually been there. "What was it like?"

"Well," said Jacques, leaning back, "you have to know that it wasn't just the students who were protesting. They got all the headlines but it was mostly the workers who shut down the country. I was one of them at the time, 18 years old and working at a lousy job in a foundry, with long hours and low pay."

"After the student protests started," he continued, "workers all over the country joined in. It was a violent time, with students and workers battling the police in the streets. At my company we went on strike and took over—kicking out the managers and locking the doors so they couldn't come back. Then I went to the center of Paris to man a barricade, ready to fight. I threw a few cobblestones and it was fun, but I'll admit that I was young and foolish then." He smiled at the memory.

"At first, nearly everyone was in favor of the strikes and protests, but then the stores started running out of food because there were no deliveries. Public transportation was on strike and gas stations were empty, so people had to walk to work. After a few weeks, everyone was fed up and turned against 'the revolution' and that ended it. "

We both sat quiet for a moment. I could tell that Jacques was reminiscing, thinking back to his life as a young man.

"Was it worth it?" I finally asked. "Would you do it again?"

"Yes and no," Jacques replied. "I think it was necessary at the time because working conditions were terrible. After the strikes, we workers received better pay and more time off. But since then I think that France has gone too far—we want too much and we aren't willing to work for it. French companies have trouble being competitive because of this."

I thought about our conversation for a long time after I got home. To actually know someone who had manned a barricade! It was kind of like knowing someone who had been at Dr. King's "I Have A Dream" speech. I wondered if I knew anyone else who'd been at the protests and thought of Marie-France and Xavier. I decided I'd ask them the next time we got together.

I had the opportunity a couple of weeks later, when Val and I dropped by for a cup of coffee. Xavier was away for a few days so I couldn't ask him, but Marie-France was there and I asked if she had been a student protester.

"Oh, yes," she said, her eyes shining, "it changed my life!"

"Changed your life?" I said. "How?"

"I was going to college then," Marie-France replied, "and working part-time, but then my company went on strike so I didn't have a job. I heard the police were beating students and I was shocked. That could have been me! I wasn't very political but I knew I had to get involved."

"I joined a group of students and we built a barricade near the main battles. We had a big pile of cobblestones to throw at the police but they never came close enough. It was exciting—fun actually! I left after a few days because it started to become too dangerous and we ran out of food."

"That sounds scary," I said. "Were you glad you did it?"

"Oh, yes!" said Marie-France. "After the protests I felt like I could do whatever I wanted and I could make my own decisions, which was unusual for a woman at the time. I went to India and lived there for a while, as a way to express my newfound sense of freedom." Her expression became a little dreamy. "For people my age, May '68 was an explosion of joy and hope. The 60s were a time when we felt there was more and more freedom in our lives, with rock music and the birth control pill and things like that, and this was the culmination of it all. It really did change my life."

Talking to Marie-France and Jacques helped me understand why May '68 still has such a hold on the French imagination. It was a huge, violent event that marked an era, with rioting in the streets and a government teetering on the edge of collapse. And it was also an inspiring one, with the powerless standing up against the powerful and actually winning.

Some French people, like Marie-France, still see it in idealist, almost romantic, terms. Others like Jacques take a more pragmatic view, tallying up the positives and negatives. But that's not surprising—if you asked Americans whether the antiwar protests of the 1960s were a good or a bad thing, you'd get a range of views as well.

Every society is complex, France no less than any other, and every day I seem to find another opportunity to dive into that complexity. Talking about sports one minute, and the next minute talking about one of the most important events of the last fifty years? It's what I appreciate the most about living in this new country—every day is an adventure. And the more I learn, the more I see the world through French eyes.

A New Challenge

Life in Provence is slower paced than in California, a lot slower, and Val and I relax more when we're there. No more rushing from one meeting to another, or hurrying to answer every email, or stressing out from being stuck in traffic. Provence moves at the pace of the seasons rather than the speed of the Internet and every time we arrive and see all the vineyards and olive groves, we feel the tension seep out of our bodies.

We embrace the slower pace by going for long walks in the countryside, taking the time to appreciate the nature around us. We hear birds singing in the trees and stop to listen to them for a while. There are wild herbs everywhere—fragrant thyme and pungent rosemary—and Val will often pick a few sprigs on our walks. "I'll use these for dinner tonight," she'll say. When I'm in Provence I feel connected to the land in a way I never do back home.

One of our favorite walks is up to La Caume, the highest point in the Alpilles. We follow a trail that meanders through pine forests and green meadows, with boulders scattered here and there. One time we heard bells clanking ahead of us and were mystified by the sound until we turned a corner and came across a flock of sheep.

Their guard dog spotted us and raced over, eyes alert for danger, but we must have passed muster because after a few sniffs he lost interest and ran back to his sheep. On the far side of the flock we could see the shepherd leaning against his staff. It's one of the things that make Provence so special, the way we occasionally stumble across a scene that hasn't changed for centuries.

The trail eventually starts climbing and we begin to see St-Rémy below, then as we get higher still we see Avignon surrounded by its ramparts. When we reach the top, winded but exhilarated, the views are magnificent in all directions.

Look! There's the massive tower of Tarascon, guarding the Rhône River. Look! There's Mont

Sainte-Victoire, the one Cézanne painted over and over. On a clear day we can see the blue waters of the Mediterranean Sea, sparkling in the sun. If there's a better view in Provence, I haven't found it.

Another favorite walk is along the base of the Alpilles, out to an old Roman bridge. We go past vineyard after vineyard, with old gnarled vines that produce the wines we enjoy so much. Along the way we pass a small airport where we like to stop for a cool drink of water and watch gliders take off. Sometimes one will fly above us as it comes in for a landing—we don't see it coming, just hear a gentle swooshing sound overhead.

We also bike in the rugged Alpilles, to places like the *Val d'Enfer* (Hell Valley). It's a rocky, sunbaked valley of austere beauty near the top of the mountains, so getting there is no easy thing. The first time we tried it our ride started easily enough but then we turned left onto a road that looked, oh, about straight up.

"Are you sure we want to do this?" I asked Val.

"Of course," she said. "Don't be a wuss."

So we took the road and started pedaling. Up, up, up, through vineyards and forests. What a climb! Further and further we went, our lungs on fire. We stopped periodically to catch our breath and massage our legs. Up, up, up. Long minutes ticked by.

At this point we had gone about half a mile.

The day was getting hotter and the only breeze was from all the other bikers whizzing by. They would pass us with a friendly call of *Courage!* and a look of concern on their faces.

Up, up, up we biked, going slower and slower. Two old ladies passed us on their bikes. Then a couple walking their dog. And a guy using a cane. Seriously, I thought, we've got to get in better shape. We eventually gasped our way to the top and were rewarded with a spectacular view across the valley to the medieval village of Les Baux.

Encouraged by our success, we started riding up to the *Val d'Enfer* more and more often. We slowly got stronger and had to stop less often. Then one day Val came up with one of her crazy ideas.

"We should ride to the other side!" she said. There's no stopping Val; she's always looking for a new challenge.

Let's just say I didn't embrace the idea right away. "You realize," I replied, "that means we have to climb up and over the Alpilles *twice*, right? Because once we make it to the other side, we have to come back." I can read a map, after all.

"Sure," she said, "so we'll stop and have lunch in the middle."

Well that got my attention. One of our favorite restaurants is in Maussane, on the other side of the Alpilles. Val convinced me that lunch would restore our strength enough for a second ascent, so I foolishly agreed.

Conditions were perfect on the day of our ride, sunny and clear. Our ride was easy at first but then the wind picked up. Sometimes it was at our backs but usually in our faces. Only grim determination carried us forward—that and a bar of chocolate.

After what seemed like hours we made it to Maussane and the restaurant. It has a delightful terrace and we ate outside under the warm sun. The day's special was *lapin à la moutarde*, a classic rabbit dish, with *pommes dauphinoise*. Those plus a *tarte tatin* for dessert would certainly give us the strength to make it home.

After a leisurely lunch and a double espresso, we were ready for the ride back. It started out ok but that darned mountain seemed to get steeper and steeper the further we went. We thought about stopping but it's not like you can call a taxi when you're out in the sticks and have two bikes with you.

We finally made it home, exhausted but with a feeling of satisfaction. Val and I like taking on challenges big and small, and we were proud of having met this one. We talked about how we should reward ourselves.

Dessert, we decided. This was definitely going to be a two-dessert day.

Dressing In French

One thing that keeps me from becoming more French is the way I look. Oh sure, I've learned some of the classic French gestures, like the Gallic Shrug (raised shoulders, open palms and downturned corners of mouth, meaning "but what can be done?") And *Mon* œil ("my eye") which is a lower eyelid pulled down ever-so-slightly to indicate "yeah, right." But I still look American, very American, with my Levis and baggy shorts and baseball cap.

I decided one day that I needed help to look more French, so I went shopping at Decathlon. This French sporting good chain carries a wide variety of clothing and I bought a bunch—now I wear their shorts and hats and pullovers almost every day. A friend told me that Decathlon clothing is worn everywhere in France but hardly anywhere else, so when a French person travels abroad and sees someone wearing it, they know that person is French. It's kind of like a secret handshake.

But for a long time there was something still missing: scarves. I could never look French until I mastered scarves. French people wear them year-round and they wear them everywhere—I've even heard of gym instructors wearing scarves while leading exercise classes. And they wear them so elegantly that it seems instinctive; Val thinks maybe French people have a special gene for it.

When I was growing up, my experience with scarves was pretty much this: they're for the snow. You put on your big coat, wool cap, gloves and heavy scarf and head out into the cold. Scarves are protection against the elements and there's nothing elegant about them.

I had so much to learn.

Luckily, my goddaughter has French heritage and one day when she was visiting I asked her to show me how to tie a scarf. It was just a basic style, nothing special, but it was definitely French. So now I've started wearing scarves a lot.

Near St-Rémy is the village of Eygalières and it has a weekly market where we sometimes go shopping. There are a couple of fruit and vegetable stands, a fish guy, two olive sellers, a lady selling spices and another selling honey, a chicken roasting stand, a cheese monger, a butcher, and all the other vendors you'd expect to see at an outdoor market. Plus it has something you only find in France: the Scarf Man.

I love going to the Scarf Man because he has such a wide selection. He has delicate chiffon and heavy wool. He has cotton, he has linen, he has silk. There are scarves for women, for men, for kids, in all the colors of the rainbow. And there are new models every year, to keep the inventory up to date. I've seen him so many times that I've started thinking of him as my personal Scarf Man.

Soon after we arrive in Provence every year, usually in March when it's still cold, we go to the Eygalières market so I can see the Scarf Man.

"Hello," I'll say, "and happy new year!" You'd think it's too late to wish someone a happy new year, but in France it's allowed if it's the first time you see someone during the year.

"Happy new year to you," he'll reply. "How was your trip from America?" We'll chat for a while and then get down to business.

"I need a new scarf for the season," I'll say. "What do you have in your spring lineup?"

He'll lay out a dozen or so new models and then say, "Remind me, please, what you already have."

"Let's see," I'll say, "I have the dark blue one with the stripes, the light blue one with the squiggles, the black one, the grey pinstripe one, the beige one with the dots and the rose one I'm wearing right now."

"Ah yes," he'll say, "I remember now. Let me show you one I think you'll like..."

One day I learned something surprising about the French, and from Bill Nye of all people. You might know "Bill Nye The Science Guy" from his TV shows. He's the goofy fellow in the bow tie who's always explaining things like asteroids and magnetism and why volcanoes erupt. But you wouldn't think of a Science Guy as someone who would give you deep insight into the French. You would expect that to be Existentialism Guy or maybe the Postmodernism Guy, but no.

The *New York Times* interviewed Nye for their Travel section (he flies a lot and is known as a spectacularly organized packer). The *Times* reporter asked him, "What do you always take with you when you travel?" Nye described the sorts of nerdy things you'd expect, like gaffer tape and dongles. But then he said something I didn't expect.

"There's a technology that allows you to deal with changes in the weather," he said. "The first and main technological innovation is a scarf. A scarf will buy you 15 degrees Fahrenheit."

"Aha!" I thought. "So *that's* why the French always wear scarves." I thought it had to do with fashion, with the French sense of style, with that *je ne sais quoi* for which the French are so famous. But no, Nye had revealed that it's really about energy efficiency.

Politicians around the world are always prattling on about how we need a Green Economy. They wax poetic about solar panels, smart grids, and millions of new jobs, while very little actually happens. But while others talk, the French act.

France has quietly built a dominant market position in one of the most important green industries of the future, and the evidence is literally in front of our eyes. Think about it: the French wear scarves year-round. AND they know how to tie them. A properly tied scarf serves a dual purpose: not only does it look good but it undoubtedly also increases the "thermal yield." Clever, those French.

The results are clear—France is much more energy efficient than the United States. And more stylish, to boot.

Hermes: World Leader in Greentech. Who knew?

Living History

World War II may have ended long ago but it's still living history in France. Every ten years, for example, France holds a huge commemoration of the invasion of Normandy, attended by heads of state from around the world plus a dwindling number of veterans.

A friend gave me a book about WWII by a French historian to help me understand it from a French perspective. I was fascinated by how parochial the French view of the war was. France didn't fight in the Pacific, so that was barely mentioned. Pearl Harbor? Hiroshima? Nope, not a word.

But as I thought about it, I realized that America has its own parochial view. I was raised during the Cold War, when "those commies in Russia" were the bad guys, so I never heard about their tremendous sacrifices in WWII. Instead, I learned about the Battle of the Bulge and things like that. Sure, some other countries might have helped out here and there, but the war pretty much began on D-Day and we Americans were the heroes—Yay, America! That's our national myth.

And now I learned that France has its own national myth, one that avoids the inconvenient truth that the French government collaborated shamefully with the Nazis. Sure, there was the famous French Resistance but not many people were actually in it.

After France was liberated, the country was badly divided and there was a risk of civil war, so Charles de Gaulle came up with a myth to pull the country together. Yes, he said, there had been a few bad *pommes* during the war, but every other man, woman and child had supported the Resistance at risk of life and limb. Yay, France! It's no surprise that this myth turned out to be very popular.

I was interested in both the myth and the reality of the war and so I was thrilled when the local historical society organized a talk called *The Resistance in St-Rémy*. The event was held at the town's movie theater and it was so full that Val and I had to hunt around to find two seats together.

"Maybe it's because Jean Moulin was from around here," I said. Moulin was a top Resistance leader and today is a national hero.

The speaker that evening was a historian and specialist on the war. He started with some background information and then posed a surprising question.

"How many women were in the Resistance?" he asked, then paused so people could ponder the question.

"We used to think there were very few," he continued, "because after the war, when the government compiled their official figures, the question they asked was, 'Who fought using guns?' And because most of the fighters were men, the idea took hold that men made up most of the Resistance."

"Then in the 1980s a new generation of historians took a closer look at the question. Instead of asking, 'Who carried a gun?' they asked 'Who risked their life?' Ah, that is a much better question. It allows us to include couriers, nurses, and those who sheltered fighters and traveled after curfew. While no definitive figures exist, it's now clear that an important part of the Resistance was made up of women."

He paused again to let that sink in. You could see people in the audience look at each other like they were thinking, "Yup, that makes sense."

Then the historian really got our attention. "I have a document to share with you, one that was only recently discovered. It's a list of the *actual members of the Resistance* in St-Rémy." The room started buzzing. He put a copy of the document on a big projector—a list of names written in old-fashioned handwriting. Everyone in the audience stared intently, looking for ones they recognized.

"This is a short list, as you can see," he said. "St-Rémy had a wartime population of about 6,000 and there are only 52 names here. And of those 52, how many were women? The number is 26—exactly half."

The buzz in the audience got louder. I could see a few women kind of poke their husbands like they were saying, "See, we're just as good as you."

The historian took questions from the audience for a while and then the presentation ended with a bang.

"And now I have a special guest to introduce to you."

The historian told us that one of the 26 women was still alive and was in the audience that night. Now in her 90s, she had been a teenager during the war and had bravely worked with her father to smuggle guns and messages at night. The penalty for getting caught? Summary execution.

When the lady was introduced and slowly walked to the center of the stage, the audience leapt to its feet and showered her with applause. She stood by the microphone for several moments, seemingly overwhelmed by all the attention. Then she cleared her throat and the room fell silent.

"Thank you," she said softly. "I don't know that what I did was heroic, I just know it was necessary." She paused and blinked a few times, as if fighting back tears. "Let us hope that such dark days never return." She stopped and blinked again, then took a deep breath. "*Vive la France!*"

You don't see a real hero every day. It was inspiring to be in the presence of one.

The Art Of Débat

The phone rang and it was Marie-France, inviting us to lunch on Friday.

"I'll make *le grand aïoli,*" she said. "It's a traditional dish that you have to try. Sophie and Jacques are coming, too, so it will be a lovely afternoon."

"Of course!" I said. "We'll be there!"

Marie-France is a talented cook and a meal at her house is always a treat. There's nothing we enjoy more than spending time with our friends over a long meal, talking about anything and everything, and this time there would be a new twist. We were intrigued by *le grand aïoli,* something we had heard about but never tried. Once again, Marie-France was introducing us to a Provençal specialty and we couldn't wait.

When Friday rolled around, we had to decide what to bring as a gift for our hosts. It didn't have to be much, but it's an important French custom to bring something like wine, flowers or chocolate.

"Should I raid the *cave* and bring a bottle from Gigondas?" I asked Val.

"Good idea," she said, "and I picked up some *fraises du bois* at the market this morning so I'll bring a basket of those, too." *Fraises du bois* are wild strawberries that are only available for a few weeks in April, much smaller than the regular kind and very sweet.

Friday's weather was warm so we had our *apéro* on the old stone veranda overlooking the garden. Marie-France has an extremely green thumb and her big backyard is full of lush trees and all kinds of flowering plants. Every year we help out with her cherry harvest, racing to gather the fruit before the neighborhood birds eat it all.

As I settled into my chair, I felt something brush my leg and looked down to see a cat walking by. Xavier loves cats and every stray in the neighborhood knows he's a soft touch for a bowl of milk. "Hello *minette*," he said, as he leaned over to scratch the cat behind the ears.

Marie-France came out of the house carrying a big tray of appetizers, then went back in and brought out another. "And now we begin!" she announced, as we all reached for something good to eat.

The appetizers weren't fancy but, as usual, they were delicious—Marie-France had sliced baguettes into little disks and put all kinds of different toppings on them. Some had *tapenade*, that Provençal mix of chopped olives and anchovies. Others were topped with ham and the tiny French pickles called *cornichons*. My favorites were the ones with *foie gras* and a dollop of Marie-France's homemade fig jam.

As we ate our way through Marie-France's handiwork, Jacques poured us champagne from a winery where he has a special connection. In his younger days he helped harvest grapes there and still receives the "family discount." We're happy he does because who doesn't love champagne?

As we enjoyed our *apéro*, Xavier told us about his upcoming photography exhibition.

"I call it *In The Footsteps of Rimbaud*," he said. "Everyone knows that Rimbaud was a great French poet, maybe the greatest, but not many people know that he lived much of his life in

Ethiopia. I traveled the country and took pictures of the places where he lived and worked." He passed around some of the photos and we all agreed they were beautiful.

As we drained our glasses and finished the appetizers, Marie-France said she had a story to tell. She turned towards Val and me.

"And now I'll explain *le grand aïoli,*" she said.

We sat up straighter and paid attention. I hoped there wouldn't be a quiz.

"France has been a Catholic country for centuries," she said, "and for most of that time we weren't allowed to eat meat on Fridays, so fish became the traditional Friday meal. But this is Provence and there's a lot more here than just fish. No, here we have magnificent produce of all kinds and we especially love our garlic! So our ancestors combined them into the Friday tradition of Provence, *le grand aïoli.*"

Aïoli, she explained, is a thick, pungent mayonnaise. Cloves of fresh garlic are ground in a mortar to create a paste, and then eggs and oil are added and briskly mixed together. Because local farm eggs have such dark orange yolks, the *aïoli* comes out a bright yellow rather than the sickly off-white of a typical grocery store mayo.

"*Aïoli* is a dish that you may have had before," Marie-France continued, "and a delicious one. But *le grand aïoli* is an entire meal. You'll see."

She went into the house and came back staggering under the weight of the biggest marble mortar I've ever seen. It must have been a foot across and was overflowing with its aromatic prize. "*Voila!*" she said. "*L'aïoli!*"

Now Marie-France and Xavier both went inside and came back with two huge platters of food. I counted at least half a dozen kinds of steamed vegetables, plus hard-boiled eggs and filets of salt cod. Val and I stared in amazement at all the food—we could see why it's called *grand*. We all loaded up our plates, along with healthy dollops of the *aïoli*, and dipped bites of cod, green beans, fennel, and everything else into that vivid yellow mayonnaise. It was garlic heaven.

Xavier had put me in charge of the wine and I'd poured out a glass for everyone when the food came out. But we were all talking and eating so enthusiastically that I forgot to refill them. Jacques cleared his throat. "Keith," he said, "*les mouches ont pieds*," and gave his empty glass a knowing look.

"Wait...what?" I asked. We had been speaking French all afternoon but I didn't understand what Jacques had said. Something about feet?

"It means 'the flies have feet,'" he explained. "My glass is so dry that if one flew in, it wouldn't be able to swim. It would have to walk on its tiny feet." In other words, *refill my glass!* It reminded me of another expression he once taught me that means the same thing, *la mer est basse* ("the tide is out").

We were having one of those perfect French afternoons, eating and drinking and enjoying each other's company, when Val decided to toss in a bomb.

"So what does everyone think of Edward Snowden?" she asked brightly.

"Edward Snowden!" I thought. "Not him!" I considered diving under the table to avoid the explosion.

In case you've forgotten, Snowden is a former US intelligence officer who revealed a bunch of government secrets and then fled to Russia. For the prior few months there had been one shocking revelation after another that made headlines around the world. *US spies on its citizens! US illegally collects phone records! US taps German leader's cellphone!* Each one was met with outrage.

And what was this week's big story? *US spies on France!* It dominated the French news and people across the country were up in arms. I feared the same reaction here, with Val and me being pummeled as the representatives of an evil empire. But it wasn't like that at all.

Our discussion was long and energetic and sometimes emotional, as you might expect, and Marie-France had especially strong feelings.

"Remember what we did to the Jews," she said. "That must never happen again!"

During the war, the Vichy regime used government records to identify Jews and send them to their deaths. So anything that smacks of government invasion of privacy draws an understandably strong reaction in France.

"But let's also remember the terrorists!" countered Jacques. "Sometimes we have to give up some privacy to protect our security."

Everyone joined in and sometimes we all talked at once. There were arguments and counterarguments about whether Snowden was telling the truth, about when and how spying is justified, about whether the *New York Times* is more or less biased than *Le Figaro*.

What surprised me about our *débat*—and it was a big surprise, given such a hot topic—was that it never became personal. There were strong feelings and occasionally raised voices, but somehow it stayed at the level of ideas. I'd seen people arguing like this before, in cafes or the town square, but never been in the middle of it myself.

Now I was able to see how good the French are at disagreeing. My friends were able to attack one another's *ideas* but not *each other*. In the US, such strong differences of opinion too often turn personal. Arguments can damage friendships and even split families. But here, our energetic discussion hadn't hurt our friendship—maybe it had even made it stronger.

And the hot emotions didn't linger. After we had all had our say, it was time to move on and talk about something else.

"Who's ready for dessert?" Marie-France asked, as she began to clear the table. "And Sophie, you must tell us about your daughter's new boyfriend."

I Want To Be A Fonctionnaire

When you live in two countries like Val and I do, you often find yourselves comparing them. It's not so much that one is better than the other, they're just different and the differences can be illuminating. We often find ourselves playing a game of "compare the countries" with Sophie and Jacques, and one of our favorite topics is the way each country conducts business.

"If you want a good career in France," Jacques once told us, "you have to go to a *grande école*."

Grande École means Top School, and it's not surprising that a degree from one of them is valuable. After all, in the US, "Princeton" opens more doors than "State College." But I was shocked by how big an advantage a Top School degree gives you in France and how long the advantage lasts.

"Let me give you example," Jacques said. "I was rebellious when I was young and it took me years to get my act together. I eventually earned an engineering degree and worked my way up to a senior position in one of France's largest companies. But my school wasn't famous and so I didn't have one of those prestigious degrees."

"Right before I retired, there was another guy who had the same job I did. We were the same age and both did good work, so we should have been paid about the same. But no, my colleague made more than me, much more, because I only went to an average school and he went to *Polytechnique*."

Jacques was referring to *L'École Polytechnique*, perhaps the grandest of all the *grandes écoles*. It's famous as the breeding ground of French presidents and corporate titans. *Polytechnique* began as a military academy under Napoleon and its students sometimes parade through Paris wearing 19th century army uniforms.

"Because the other guy graduated from *Polytechnique*, even though it was decades ago, he earned twice as much as me. *Twice as much!* For doing the same job."

It reminded me of a story my friend Thierry told me, kind of the same thing but from the other side. Thierry not only graduated from one of the most important *grandes écoles,* he also earned a top score on an important national exam. When he graduated, a big company offered him a very high starting salary.

"But that's not all," Thierry said, "the company also told me what my salary would be five, ten, even fifteen years in the future. Can you imagine that?"

"I asked how my pay would change if I did a good job or a bad job and they were astonished that I would ask such a question. They told me that it wouldn't change at all because the only things that mattered were my degree and my test score. I didn't accept their offer because I wanted to have to prove myself every day and be rewarded if I did a good job." He's now a successful entrepreneur.

I can see that paying for the prestige of someone's degree, rather than their performance, isn't good for the French economy. It might be one of the reasons so many talented French people emigrate—tens of thousands of them work near us in California, drawn by the opportunities to succeed or fail. And there are so many French expatriates in London that it's sometimes called "the fifth largest city in France."

Taking a big risk in search of a big reward is uncommon in France because failure is punished. In Silicon Valley, lots of people join startup companies that fail, but that's ok because it's considered a good learning experience. In France, as in many European countries, if you work for a failed startup it's a scarlet letter that can haunt the rest of your career.

That may be why a majority of French college students said recently that their ideal job was *fonctionnaire* (government bureaucrat). *Fonctionnaires* have job security, lots of vacation, and generous pensions—who wouldn't like that? Plus they're famous for...how can I put this?...*not working very hard*. That last part makes them the butt of jokes, like the one Xavier told me about three kids discussing what time their parents get home from work.

"My dad works for L'Oréal," says the first. "His job ends at 5:00 and he takes the train, so he gets home at 6:00."

"My mom works for Renault," says the second. "Her job also ends at 5:00 and she takes the Métro, so she gets home at 5:30."

"My dad works for the government," says the third. "His job ends at 5:00 too, so he gets home at 4:30."

And then there's this one.

One *fonctionnaire* complains to another, "I have a new boss and now I can't sleep on the job anymore."

"Why?" asks the second. "Because he keeps an eye on you?"

"No, because he snores!"

And here's my favorite joke, about the *fonctionnaire* and the genie.

One day a *fonctionnaire* is in his office, doing nothing as usual. As he sits with his feet up on his desk, he notices something behind a stack of old papers. He walks over and picks it up.

"Hm, it's some kind of lamp," he says to himself. "I'll take it home and put it on my mantle."

That night he takes the lamp out of his briefcase and sees how dirty it is.

"I need to clean this," he thinks, so he finds a cloth and starts rubbing. Suddenly there's a loud POOF! and a genie appears.

"Thank you, master, for releasing me from my prison," says the genie. "In gratitude I grant you three wishes."

The *fonctionnaire* thinks for a moment.

"For my first wish, I want to be the most handsome man in the world."

POOF!

The *fonctionnaire* runs to the mirror. Looking back at him is a man more handsome than Yves Montand and George Clooney combined. He's so excited he can hardly contain himself.

"For my second wish, I want to be on a tropical island, surrounded by beautiful women."

POOF!

The *fonctionnaire* suddenly feels warm sand between his toes and hears waves lapping softly at the shore of a lush tropical island. All around him are bikini-clad beauties, gazing at him with desire in their eyes. His knees get weak.

"For my final wish, I never want to have to work again."

POOF!

He's back in his office.

Bulls Go For A Swim

"The bull has escaped!"

Val and I looked up to see a thousand pounds of anger barreling down the street right at us. We ran to safety as the bull thundered past, followed by French cowboys on horseback. It was a terrifying moment, the kind you never forget.

South of St-Rémy lies the famously wild Camargue, a vast, marshy territory that is home to pink flamingos and white horses running free. This is where the *gardians* live, the French cowboys who form a living link to France's romantic past. And there are bulls, lots of bulls.

Every region of France has its own customs, sometimes even its own language, and it's one of the most fascinating aspects of the country. One of the things that makes our corner of Provence unique is its bulls and we see signs of them everywhere, from the *Croix de Camargue* bumper stickers (it's the symbol of the *gardians*) to the popular men's shirts with little bulls printed on them. Val and I dig into this aspect of local culture every chance we get, figuring that the more we understand it the more we'll understand the region.

One way that young Provençal men demonstrate their bravery is in the local sport called *Course Camarguaise*. Some people call this French bullfighting but it's not fighting at all and the bulls aren't hurt. Instead, doodads are tied around their horns and the brave young men, the *raseteurs*, have to run up to the bulls and take off the doodads. It's a popular event, filling arenas throughout Provence, and we go several times a year. Val loves the sport, mostly because the *raseteur's* traditional outfit includes what she calls "those tight white pants."

One day we took Sophie to a *Course* after she told us she had never been to one. It was gratifying to be able to introduce a bit of French culture to someone who'd lived in France nearly her entire life.

It was in Arles, in the old Roman amphitheater, and it seemed like the whole town turned out for the event. Every restaurant and bar was full and revelers milled through the streets. Thousands of spectators packed the arena and the afternoon began with a program of traditional music and culture. First came the *gardians* on horseback, slowly cantering in formation. Then it was the brave *raseteurs*, strutting into the arena in their white pants and waving to the crowd. Val sat up straighter when she saw them.

The grand finale came when the ladies of Arles strolled in, decked out in their elegant *arlésienne* costumes. These are long, colorful dresses, usually silk, topped with white lace scarves over the shoulders. Family jewelry accents the outfit and it's topped by a dainty hat placed primly on pinned-up hair. The people of Provence are fiercely proud of these traditional costumes and we often see ladies wearing them at village festivals.

Finally, the *Course* began and Sophie noticed that a grizzled old fellow in front of us was keeping score. There were eight bulls that day, one after the other, and he put stars next to each one. The first bull got three stars but the next few only got zeroes.

"You didn't like these bulls, Monsieur?" Sophie asked him.

"They're only good for sausage," he growled.

Eventually he started giving higher scores because the best bulls had been saved for the end. The final bull was a monster, bigger and meaner than the other ones. He charged into the arena and started pawing the ground, showering spectators with sand. The *raseteurs* looked nervous and suddenly became very polite; I couldn't tell what they were saying but I was sure it was something like this.

"Please, you go first."

"Oh, no, I couldn't possibly. Please, after you."

The old guy gave this bull a full ten stars.

Sometimes there's an *Abrivado* the day before a *Course*, and it's an exciting event in itself. At an *Abrivado*, a bull charges out of the back of a truck, ready to escape. He's met by *gardians* on horseback that have their horses in a V formation, like a flock of geese in flight. The bull charges into the center of the V and the *gardians* immediately take off, trapping the bull and leading him to the arena.

To be able to do this—controlling a bull with nothing more than horses and without being gored—is a real test of horsemanship that only the best *gardians* can pass. But when a bull escapes, you can be sure they don't get top marks.

The day the bull escaped and almost ran over Val and me, I heard one guy say to his neighbor, "Those guys need a lot of practice."

"They shouldn't even call themselves *gardians,*" said the neighbor. "They should be riding ponies!"

Then there's the *Gaso de Taureaux*, where bulls swim across a lake. I don't know why—maybe they need to freshen up a bit.

When Val and I went to our first *Gaso*, it was at a lake that was skinny at one end, maybe fifty yards wide. *Gardians* would run bulls four at a time toward this skinny bit, then stop and pull their horses to the side at the last moment. The unsuspecting bulls would plunge into the water and swim to the other side, where they would be corralled by more *gardians*.

Two ropes marked the path across the lake and there were dozens of people floating in boats next to them, with hundreds more people on shore. Sausages were grilled, wine was drunk, and bands played—the crowd even did the wave. Everyone was having a good time and we joined right in.

The first group of bulls went off without a hitch. Tons of bull, horse and *gardian* came charging towards the lake, then the horses pulled over and screeched to a halt while the bulls kept going and swam to the other side. Success!

The second group didn't go quite as well. This time one of the horses forgot to stop and ran into the lake and swam along with the bulls. His poor *gardian* fell into the water and clung desperately to the saddle, surrounded by thrashing bulls and looking very nervous. Somehow he climbed back aboard his horse as it left the lake.

And then there was the third group. Everything was fine at first, but when the bulls were halfway across the lake they decided to make a break for it. The four huge beasts with their sharp horns made a sudden left turn, bursting through the line of boats and scattering the spectators. They swam toward open water while a boat full of drunken fools gave chase—one guy even jumped on a bull and rode bareback for a while. At first we could see the bulls' heads and tails as they swam to freedom, but as they receded further and further into the distance all we could see were tall horns bobbing along.

Luckily, the fire department was prepared for this, with a speedboat at the ready and several steely-eyed *pompiers* (firemen) geared up for action. But they had neglected to prime the engine ahead of time and spent precious minutes swearing and trying to start it while the bulls continued their escape. Eventually, the engine fired up and the *pompiers* roared off.

Val looked at me. "Bulls making a getaway in a lake—who would believe it?" she said. "Boy, do I feel a long way from home. Everything there is predictable and kind of sanitized, but here it's so wild and so...*real*."

Yes, it was wild and real. And it was fun. Here we were, eating our sausages and drinking our wine and cheering for the *gardians* along with the locals. It was funny because we felt far from home but we also felt comfortable, like we were *at home* at the same time. Were we finally settling in?

The Real Provence

I was standing in line at the bank and it wasn't moving. Maybe there was a computer problem or maybe it was something else, but all I knew was that I'd been standing there for a long time. I was starting to think that I should come back later when the lady in front of me gave out an exasperated sigh and said, "*Mince, c'est le temps de tuer un âne à coup de figues!*" Everyone else in line turned to her and nodded vigorously.

I didn't understand what she said but I caught the words for donkey and fig. Maybe it was a local expression? I asked Marie-France about it the next time I saw her.

"It's probably this," she said, and repeated the expression. "It's one of my favorites, very Provençal. It means that something is taking so long that you have enough time to kill a donkey just by throwing figs at it. And if you know how soft figs are and how tough donkeys are, that's a very long time."

Living in Provence lets me pick up these colorful expressions from time to time, like when Jacques was complaining about an acquaintance who is a real tightwad.

"Every time we meet at a café for a drink or a cup of coffee," he said, "we talk and tell stories and have a fun time together. But when it comes to paying the bill, he never offers to chip in. Here in Provence we say he has *oursins dans la poche*—sea urchins in his pocket. They prevent him from reaching in there for his wallet."

Another time Xavier warned me that I should never call someone *brave*. I was confused because *brave* means brave.

"Yes, it's true that in other parts of France, if someone calls you brave it's a compliment," Xavier explained. "But here in Provence if someone calls you *brave*, or even worse *bien brave*, they're saying that you are nice but not very bright. So be careful how you use that word."

Learning all these expressions reminds me that language is one of the things that make Provence unique. Food is another, dishes like *le grand aïoli* and *bouillabaisse*. And what could be better than the thirteen desserts the good people of Provence eat at Christmas?

Then there are the traditions that set Provence apart, like the melon festival in Cavaillon. And the annual blessing of the truffles at the church in Richerenches. And the celebration of the day Saint Gens poked two fingers in a rock and water miraculously burst forth from one hole and wine from the other.

Provence has other traditions as well, scary ones, like the legend of the Tarasque. The story is told that thousands of years ago a terrible monster lived in the depths of the Rhône River. He came out periodically to sink a boat or destroy a village, carrying away screaming humans to devour in his watery lair. The local people tried to kill the Tarasque but it was too powerful and everyone lived in fear.

Then Saint Martha came along to save the day. After one of the monster's attacks, she went to the village where it was still rampaging and approached the horrible beast. As the Tarasque prepared to make Martha his next victim, she calmly raised her arms straight out, making the sign of the holy cross for all to see. At this, the fearsome beast grew afraid and cowered before Martha, weak and helpless, and the villagers finished him off. Today the town of Tarascon still carries the monster's name and a church there is said to hold the bones of the blessed saint.

Beyond the foods and legends and language that make Provence unique, there's the question of exactly where it is. You'd think this would be easy to figure out—just look at a map—but in some ways Provence is less about latitude and longitude and more about a state of mind.

I often hear people in Provence refer disdainfully to *le nord* (the north), which for them is pretty much anywhere in France that isn't Provence. They might say that they're going on a trip to *le nord* or that so-and-so is from *le nord*, and *le nord* isn't considered a good place—no, it's cold and rainy there and the food isn't as good as in Provence and the people aren't as noble.

If *le nord* begins at the border of Provence, then where exactly is that? This is where the state of mind comes in. Some people say it's Montélimar, only 50 miles north of us, because it marks the limit of where the Provençal language was spoken in the old days. Other people put it even further south, at Orange. And then there's Jacques, who likes to joke, "It starts at the edge of my garden."

But my favorite story is from the time we were having coffee with Sophie in St-Rémy. As the waiter came to take our order, Sophie was talking about the animals she sometimes sees in the streets of our town.

"You have bulls charging through town during the *Abrivado*," she said, "and sheep driven down the main street for the *transhumance*. And then there's the festival of Saint Eloi, when horses with flowers in their manes stroll through town. And even though I live only a few kilometers away, my village doesn't have any of those. I don't know why, maybe you do a better job of maintaining your traditions."

The waiter overheard Sophie and asked, "And where are you from, Madame?"

"Le Thor, very close to here," she replied.

"But Madame," he cried, "that's *le nord!* Of course you don't have any Provence traditions."

Sophie was so taken aback that she was speechless, while Val and I just laughed. Here we were, two Americans, and yet somehow *we* were more Provençal than her.

"Le Thor is a very nice village, Madame," continued the waiter, "but it's not Provence. It's in the *Comtat Venaissin*, a separate territory that the Pope used to own. Here is the real Provence! Remember that the great Frédéric Mistral lived here and won his Nobel Prize for writing *about us*."

When I think about all this, the local pride and the legends and the colorful expressions, I realize that much of what is essential about Provence is invisible to the eye. Visiting lavender fields and hilltop villages is a lot of fun and a delightful way to spend a vacation, but to really know Provence takes longer. It needs time to seep into you because Provence, like the best things in life, can't be rushed.

Such Good Friends

When I was in my 30s I started having stomach problems. They weren't serious but they were annoying, a sour feeling I got around lunchtime. It was a mystery until I realized that it happened when I had cereal for breakfast. It turned out that I was becoming lactose-intolerant, so I switched from regular milk to soymilk and the problem went away. I could still eat yogurt and cheese and ice cream, but that has slowly changed to the point where now I can't eat dairy products at all. So much for all that yummy French cheese.

Then one day a few years ago, my doctor told me that the results of my annual physical exam were a concern. She said that my Vitamin D was too low, even after I had started taking a supplement.

"We need to figure this out," she said. "I'm sending you to an endocrinologist." So I met with the endocrinologist and she sent me off to take a bunch of tests.

"I may have found something," the endocrinologist told me a few weeks later. "You might have celiac disease but I'm not sure because the test results are borderline. We want to be sure, so you need to see a gastroenterologist." So I met with this new doctor, who studied the test results and gave me some bad news.

"You almost certainly have celiac disease," he said. "This is a severe gluten intolerance that can be life threatening if not treated."

"But doctor," I replied, "I can't have celiac disease because bread and pasta and things like that don't bother me, so it must be something else."

The doctor looked at me and I could tell he was thinking, "Oh great, here's another guy who thinks he's a doctor. Maybe he can pay off my school loans, too!" But instead he said, "You may have silent celiac, a type without obvious symptoms but dangerous nonetheless. We have to do one more test to be sure and we'll receive the results in a few weeks."

Well, in a few weeks Val and I would be landing in Provence so we would get the results there. I took the test but I didn't believe I had a problem. I had no symptoms that I was aware of and the endocrinologist had said that my test results were borderline, so I was probably ok, right? At least that's what I hoped.

The day we arrived in Provence, I picked up a voicemail from the gastroenterologist. "The test confirms that you have celiac disease," it said. "You must immediately eliminate all gluten from your diet." Click.

Merde! Gluten is found in wheat so this meant no more croissants, no more baguettes, no more *pain au chocolat.* Here I was in France, the country with the world's best cheese and the world's best bread and couldn't have a bite of either. Thank goodness I could still drink French wine.

So now Val and I had a new challenge, figuring out how to go gluten-free. We would be starting from scratch because we hadn't done any research before leaving the US, foolishly believing I was ok. Now we would have to figure it out in France and in French. Where could we buy food I could eat? Would we still be able to go to restaurants? Was gluten-free food as tasteless as people said?

We started by learning the words for wheat (*blé*), rye (*seigle*) and barley (*orge*), the foods where gluten exists naturally. Then we started shopping at the *bio* store because they have a good selection of gluten-free products. A *bio* store is an organic food store, but not the old granola-and-Birkenstocks variety—it's more like a French version of Whole Foods where you can buy organic snails and such.

Eating at restaurants presented another challenge. It wasn't hard to avoid the usual suspects like bread, but what about hidden gluten, such as the flour used to thicken sauces? Our French was pretty good but there was still a lot to learn, like how to ask if there's the pesky additive *maltodextrine* in a dish. Over time, Val and I have figured out what dishes I can safely eat and which ones I have to avoid, but going to a restaurant still makes me a little nervous.

One thing I appreciate is that the waiters and waitresses are always helpful. They'll say things like, "Oh yes, my aunt has the same problem," or, "My neighbor can't eat gluten either." In California, going gluten-free has become a fad, but not in Provence. Who would skip delicious French bread if they didn't have to? So when I say I can't eat gluten, people take me seriously and kind of feel sorry for me.

After lots of trial and error, Val and I have figured out gluten-free living in France. We can eat at certain restaurants and Val cooks safely at home. But I still worry about being a burden to our friends, especially because a lot of our social life "revolves around the table." I'm already a problem guest because I have to avoid dairy, and adding gluten into the mix makes me about the worst dinner guest in the world. But our friends have taken my gluten problem in stride and even see it as an opportunity to try new dishes.

Shortly after I was diagnosed, Sophie and Jacques invited us over for dinner. "I'm cooking," said Jacques, "and I'll make everything safe for you."

When we got to their house we found that it was going to be an Asian-style meal, something Jacques had never cooked before. "I was bored with the old recipes," he told us, "so this was fun!"

The highlight of the meal was the starter—spring rolls wrapped in rice paper. Every single ingredient that was stuffed into those rolls, and there were a lot of them, had been carefully sliced and chopped and minced.

"My goodness, Jacques," I said, "this looks like a lot of work. How long did it take you?"

"Oh, maybe a couple of hours," he replied. He waggled a finger that I could see had a bandage on it. "And I only cut myself once!"

But the best memory is from a meal at Marie-France's. It was the usual sixsome—Marie-France, Xavier, Sophie, Jacques, Val and me. We had a long meal with lots of courses and I'm sure Marie-France spent the entire day preparing and making sure that it was safe for me to eat. I really appreciated all the work she had done.

At the end of the meal, a very satisfied Jacques stood up and proposed a toast. "Keith," he said, "this food was all so delicious that I would like to thank you for having celiac disease!"

Could you ask for better friends?

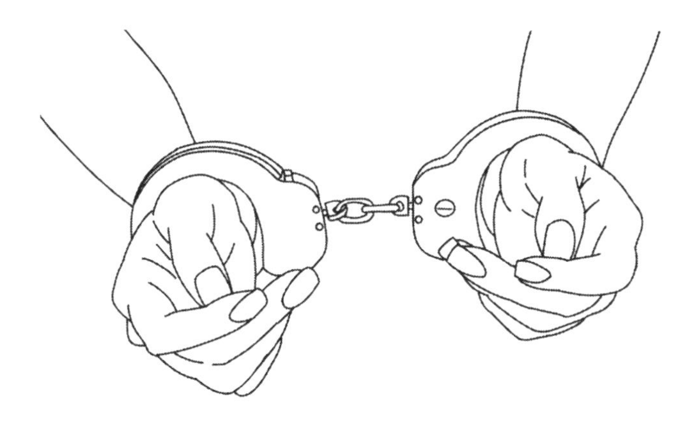

Oops

Val and I now speak reasonably good French but we still make embarrassing mistakes, like the time I booked the hotel for our first night in France. We were driving there from Zurich, where our flight from San Francisco landed, and wanted a place just inside the French border. One of the things we most look forward to is our first meal in France and we want to have it as soon as we can.

Val usually books our hotels but I volunteered to do it this time because she was busy. I could tell she was worried that I'd screw it up.

"Don't worry," I said, "I'll find us a nice place on the Interweb."

I hunted around online and found a pleasant-looking hotel called a *relais routier,* conveniently located near the freeway. I knew *relais* means "inn" and that was good enough for me because inns usually have nice restaurants. I didn't know the word *routier* but I didn't think it was important to look it up. Big mistake.

Our flight landed in the late afternoon and it was dark when we arrived at the hotel. It looked welcoming but I couldn't help noticing that the parking lot was unusually big. As in *enormous*. We carried in our luggage and then went to dinner, and when we walked into the restaurant we had to squeeze past drinkers standing three deep at the bar. They were friendly and all, but we had never seen so many people at a hotel bar before.

After we were seated, Val looked around and said, "Have you noticed that everyone here is a man?"

"Hm," I said, "I hadn't until you mentioned it but you're right. I wonder why?"

At this point the waiter came to our table to announce the dinner specials.

"Our specials tonight are hamburger with mashed potatoes, hamburger with fried potatoes and hamburger with rice," he said.

Val gave me a sharp look and I started to get nervous. What was going on here? We were in a hotel near the freeway that had a giant parking lot, an all-male clientele, and a restaurant that seemed to specialize in hamburger. Something was definitely not right and I had a feeling it had to do with *relais routier*, so I checked the dictionary on my phone. To my dismay it means...*truck stop.* So much for that delicious first dinner in France.

Note to self: Dictionaries exist for a reason.

Then there was the night Val was pulled over by the police.

We were headed home from dinner and got to where the local *gendarmes* had set up a sobriety roadblock. Every driver was being pulled over and told to blow into a breathalyzer, which meant Val because she was the one driving. I figured this would be easy because we hadn't had much to drink, but Val had other thoughts.

"I'm nervous," she said, "because I'm feeling the wine a little bit. Here, check my hand!" It was cold and clammy.

"Calm down," I said, "you'll be fine."

"But what if they put me in handcuffs and haul me off to jail? Will you know how to bail me out?"

I didn't think that I would but this was definitely not the time to point that out. "Don't worry," I said, "there's no reason to panic."

Just then a cop walked up. He was big, very big, and had a scowl on his face. He looked like someone who ate American tourists for breakfast. Now *my* hands got cold and clammy.

"Here," he growled, thrusting the breathalyzer at Val, "blow into the tube."

Val was so nervous that her usually reliable French went right out the window. She understood "blow" but missed "into the tube." She started to ask the cop to repeat himself but could only stammer out a few words, so she finally turned to the tube and sort of puffed in its general direction.

The cop was not amused.

He could tell that Val hadn't understood him so he shoved the tube at her again, pantomiming how it worked. This time she understood but didn't know that every driver received a new tube—she thought that others had already used it and there was no way she was putting that icky thing in her mouth. Instead, she just got closer and blew harder.

Now the cop got agitated. And he had a gun.

Finally, after more pantomiming and glares from the officer, Val reluctantly blew into the tube. The breathalyzer must have said we were ok because the cop grunted and sent us on our way. Val made me do all the driving for weeks after that.

And then there was the time I learned there are two parts to my brain.

We were having Sunday lunch with our friends Viviane and Gérard. It was the usual five or six hour meal and we spoke French the entire time. Towards the end, Viviane's nephew Jean-Michel came by to pick up his baby, who we had been watching for the afternoon. Jean-Michel gathered up the baby gear and was starting to leave when Viviane noticed that he had forgotten his baby bottle.

"*Tu as oublié le biberon!*" she called out, and he came back to get it. The word for "baby bottle" was one I hadn't heard before.

"Viviane, can you repeat that word for me?" I asked. "And can you spell it?"

"Sure, it's *biberon,*" she replied. "*B-i-b-e-r-o-n.* And what's it called in English?"

This was not a hard question but somehow I drew a total blank. I could see the baby bottle in Jean-Michel's hand and I knew what it was, but for the life of me I couldn't find the words. I'd been speaking so much French that I'd somehow lost my English vocabulary.

"It's called, um...it's...ah...it's, um..."

Now what were those words? Why couldn't I think of them? After several very long and embarrassing moments, I finally came up with just "bottle." Viviane thanked me but I could tell she was wondering why such a simple thing had given me a brain cramp.

It reminded me of when I read a French newspaper and then Val asks me in English what's in the news. And I can't remember! It's as if there are two parts of my brain—French and English—and I can't connect them. So during the lunch with Viviane, I was in the French part of my brain and had to struggle to find my way over to the English part. And when Val asks me in English what I've been reading in French, I can't connect the two sides.

After we got home that night, I thought about these two parts of my brain. Since I spend most of my time on the English side, I thought it would be fun to explore the French part—who knew what I'd find? Unfortunately, it turns out that the French part of my brain is filled with the same kind of useless junk that litters the English part, like the starting lineup of the 1972 Oakland A's ("Batting fourth and playing first base, Mike Epstein!")

As I poked around in the dark recesses of my French brain, I found various bits of history trivia, like the Edict of Nantes. And the opening line of the first book I ever read in French ("*Je suis né dans la ville d'Aubagne.*") Plus there were the names of some obscure French wine grapes. I even found a parking ticket from Avignon that I'd forgotten to pay.

I kept hunting around, hoping to find naughty pictures of Brigitte Bardot, but had no luck.

When Worlds Collide

After years of living part-time in France, it seems like Val and I now lead two lives, one French and one American. It's like having a split personality.

When we're in California, we live American lives. We eat meatloaf one day and tacos the next. We go to football games and cheer for our favorite team. On Thanksgiving we have turkey, on the 4th of July we watch fireworks, and all year long we grumble about those nitwits in Washington, D.C.

We love our jobs and the chance to work with smart people from all over the world. Our lives are fast-paced because Silicon Valley has an energy that's contagious, but it also has a downside—

work is demanding, rush hour traffic is terrible and there's never enough time. The level of stress can be exhilarating but also debilitating, and the high-tech game is best played when you're young because the human body can only take so much *go-go-go now-now-now*. I used to be a typical Silicon Valley maniac but I've slowed down over the years out of self-preservation.

By contrast, the relaxed pace of life is one of the things we treasure most about France, and especially Provence. When we're there, we live French lives. We slow down and spend hours around the dinner table or over a glass of wine. We appreciate the balance in French life and the emphasis on the pleasures of small things. And we're struck by how often we find ourselves talking with our friends about serious matters, subjects close to our hearts. Maybe slowing down allows them to make their way to the surface.

We had long thought of these two parts of our lives, the French and the American, as incompatible, because how do you mix fast and slow? A four-hour dinner in Provence is normal, but back home it would interfere with all those late night conference calls. And the average Silicon Valley commute would make a Provençal farmer's head explode. So rather than try to mix our two lives, we've lived them separately, each for part of the year, and enjoyed what each has to offer.

But over time our two worlds have started to blend together, bit by bit.

Of course, they were never entirely separate. When in Provence, we still exchange emails and phone calls with our family and friends back home, and we still read our hometown newspaper online. So our American life is always present, at least in the background. But for a long time the opposite wasn't true—our French life was like something we took out of a box once a year, enjoyed for a few months, and then packed up and put on a shelf.

Maybe that's because we're Americans and America is ever-present in the world, but France is less so. Stories about France are rare in US newspapers, so we had a hard time staying current on French happenings when we were back home. But then we thought, why not change that? And so we did, first by subscribing to *Le Monde,* and then to a French TV channel. Now we can keep up with French news as easily as US news.

Then we resolved to stay in better touch with our friends in Provence. We started having occasional Skype calls and they made us feel closer to them because we could see their faces when we talked. One time Sophie even showed us her new kitty on a call! We tried email, too, but that was hard because we're slow at writing in French and it took us forever to peck out what we wanted to say. Then Google Translate came along and made it easier to stay in touch, sometimes by sending quick messages to say hello. Now our French friends are in our lives even when we're far apart.

We've also brought France into our California lives by making French friends in the US. We started a local "buddy" program, matching Americans with French expats, and Val and I have become good friends with our buddies. I even made a new French friend through Skype, a language partner I talk to weekly, and because he lives near St-Rémy we get together when Val and I are in Provence.

Our two worlds collided one year, thanks to the annual *transhumance* festival. This is where thousands of sheep are herded through St-Rémy, accompanied by shepherds, dogs, and the occasional goat. It draws tourists from all over and one year they included three different couples we knew who were visiting from California.

Val and I decided to take a chance and try to mix our worlds, inviting the visiting Americans and some of our French friends to the *transhumance* and then a barbeque at our place afterwards. I'll admit that it was a risk, bringing together fourteen strangers and adding a language barrier on top of that, but we figured, why not? Some of the French spoke English and some of the Americans spoke French so there would be enough common ground if everyone made an effort.

We all met in town on the morning of the big event and Val and I kept busy making introductions and encouraging small talk. Then we watched the sheep go by, so many and so close together that it was like a river of them flowing past. The *transhumance* is an impressive sight and it made for a nice icebreaker and gave everyone something to talk about.

Then we headed to our house, where everyone pitched in to get ready. The women congregated in the kitchen and Val put them to work preparing food, while I organized the men to set up outside. We shoved two tables together, gathered chairs from inside and out, and had a lively debate about where to put the umbrellas to keep the sun off our heads. Jacques likes to grill so I put him in charge of the barbeque and soon he had a mound of sizzling lamb chops and sausages ready to eat. All this work made everyone thirsty so I assigned myself the most important job of all—opening wine bottles.

When everything was ready, we all sat down to our big French meal—lots of appetizers, Jacques' lamb chops and sausage, two kinds of quiche, a big bowl of ratatouille, a dozen baguettes, a platter of cheese, a green salad, several desserts, fruit, coffee, and plenty of wine. I stood and raised my glass. "To Franco-American friendship!" I toasted, in English and then in French. Everyone clinked glasses with their neighbors and then we all dug in. The meal went on for hours and there was lively conversation the whole time.

It was fun watching people connect in a mix of French and English. Laura and Thierry wanted to talk to each other but didn't share a common language, so Sophie stepped in and played translator. Laura would say something to Sophie in English, who would translate it into French for Thierry, who would then reply in French and have Sophie translate it back for Laura. It was like the kid's game of Telephone, but with the extra twist of two languages. Sophie must have avoided any awkward mistranslations because I never saw Thierry with a shocked look on his face or Laura storm off in a huff.

At the other end of the table, Steve and Xavier didn't share a language but they also didn't have a translator, so each tried to use the few words they knew in the other's language. They stumbled along for a while before finally giving up and communicating in a kind of sign language, with plenty of nods and smiles.

And then there were Marie-France and Gordon, each of whom is bilingual. They chatted away in English and then switched to French. Later they went back to English—talk about show offs!

After all the food, everyone needed to stretch their legs so we decided to have a *pétanque* tournament on our gravel driveway. The good thing about *pétanque* is that anyone can play—maybe not well, but even a lousy player like me can still have fun. A few of my shots were on target but most ended up in a ditch and I didn't care. Everyone else seemed to feel the same way.

As we played, drinks in hand, I looked around and took it all in. "This morning hardly anyone new each other and now it feels like I'm in a group of old friends," I thought. "The French aren't huddled on one side and the Americans on the other—we're all mixed together." If I didn't listen carefully I wouldn't even know there was a language barrier because everyone was communicating just fine.

I was sad when the sun began to set and our party came to an end. Everyone said their goodbyes with a mix of handshakes and kisses and hopes to meet again. It was as if the two worlds Val and I live in—Provence and California—had collided, mixed, and somehow melded together. Maybe they're not so different after all.

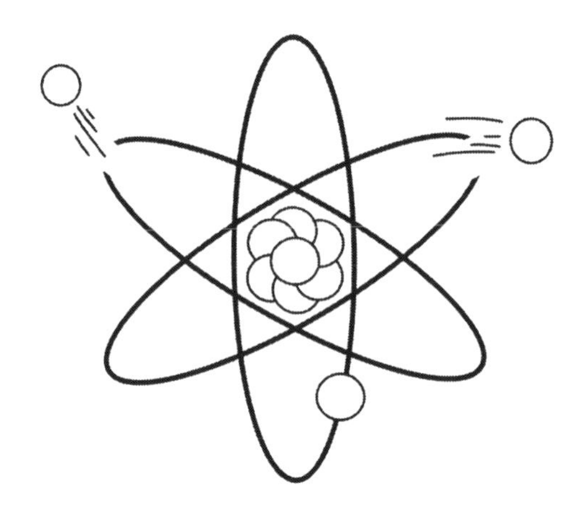

Free Electrons

When Val and I started our part-time life in Provence, we had the naïve idea—the dream really—of becoming French. And where are we now? We've certainly made a lot of progress. We speak reasonably good French and can swear enthusiastically in our new language. We've learned about French history and French politics and can work our way through entire French novels. We've adopted local sports like *Course Camarguaise*, we watch French TV, and we wear scarves at the slightest hint of cool weather. And we can complain about the government with the best of them, which is a mark of advanced Frenchness.

But will we ever make it much further? Our foreign accents are too strong to fool anyone, which means we will always stand out. People say things to us like "You speak French very well for Americans" or "You know a lot about France for Americans." While they mean well, they're also telling us that we aren't French, we're just good *for Americans*.

This means that we will forever be outsiders, welcomed into French society but only so far. No matter how hard we try, we're *étrangers*—foreigners—now and forever. But being *étrangers* has its advantages. One is that we can operate outside the normal social rules. Every country has them, these rules that govern behavior, and sometimes they can make interactions between people formal and rigid.

Val and I know the American rules but we don't know all the French rules and, as *étrangers*, we have a kind of free pass to break them—people assume we don't know any better. It's like when we accidentally use the informal *tu* form of address when we should use the formal *vous*, we're forgiven because at least we're making the effort to speak French.

Take the way we've made friends. Normally, friendship in France is supposed to progress slowly and formally because "friendship has rules." This means people begin by addressing each other only by their last names and talking only about safe subjects—books, for example, or the weather. They are supposed to keep a certain distance and refrain from showing too much enthusiasm.

Slowly, ever so slowly, by following these rules people reach the point where they can call each other by their first names. They can start to talk a bit about their personal lives—vacations, kids—and then a bit more. They can invite one another over for coffee and later for a drink. And step-by-step, over months and years, friendships are formed.

Good grief, that's way too slow for Val and me! No, we just barged right in. We started calling people by their first names right away, talked about sensitive subjects, and were wildly enthusiastic. We progressed from coffees to *apéros* to dinners in record time and now we have wonderful French friends. We got away with breaking the friendship rules because we didn't know what they were, so we just did our best and it worked. Not bad *for Americans.*

Now, even when we do know the rules, we pick and choose which ones to follow. It's like when we have guests for dinner, French protocol requires that the hostess serve food onto everyone's plate. But this makes Val uncomfortable so she just puts the food out and says, "Help yourselves!" After the initial shock, our French friends have come to like it because they can take as much of each dish as they want, rather than being subject to the whims of the hostess.

And we talk about "forbidden" subjects all the time. Politics? Our friends span the spectrum, from far left to far right, and we talk politics together for hours, often disagreeing but always in a respectful way. Religion? We've attended French baptisms and French Passover Seders and had intimate discussions with our friends about our respective faiths. Money? We all complain about taxes (of course) but we also talk about the role of money in France and the US and it has given us insight into how the countries are similar and how they're different.

Being unleashed this way makes us what the French call *électrons libres*, or free electrons. Remember back in high school when we learned about electrons that somehow escape the clutches of a molecule and happily meander about on their own? That's us. We have a freedom that's not available to French people. Our foreignness, which makes us outsiders, also gives us a certain liberty—an excuse to do what we want.

Being *électrons libres* is one of the things that make France special for us, this freedom we don't have in the US. And while we'll never be French, no matter how hard we try, we still carry a bit of France in us every day. And that's a beautiful thing.

Home

Are we the same people we were the day we first moved to Provence? We have certainly changed a lot.

The first change is that we've learned to speak a second language, not an easy thing in your 40s and 50s. Neither one of us has a talent for languages, and for me the idea of speaking French is way beyond what I ever thought I could do. It's changed the way I think about myself, almost like I'm a different person than I thought I was.

I remember one time when I was just getting started and I saw an American, a guy about my age, chatting in French with some people in a restaurant. I was amazed because what he was doing was so far beyond anything I ever imagined I could do myself. I thought, "How cool to be *that guy*, able to speak real French." It was a kind of impossible dream for me.

Then last year I was having coffee with Jacques and I noticed that an American guy at the next table kept looking at me. He could tell I was American (we Yanks can always spot each other) and I think he was intrigued by my French conversation. Suddenly I realized that I had achieved my impossible dream and become *that guy*. It kind of blew my mind.

People ask us if we're fluent in French and we say, "We're conversational." We can share perspectives with other people and make a human connection. We can communicate and that's what we care about. And the language has embedded itself deeply enough in our brains that when we spend an entire day in French, never speaking a word of English, we don't get ridiculously tired like we used to.

Being able to speak French, even imperfectly, has been the key that has opened up a new world for us. Without it, we would be like some of the foreigners who live in France, able to be there... but not fully. Learning the language has allowed us to make new friends and immerse ourselves in the daily life of a new land.

Doing so has given us a wider perspective on the world. The French often look at things differently than we do in the US. It's like when Marie-France took such a strong stand on the right to privacy. Americans believe in a right to privacy, too, but not as intensely because our history is different. And Americans see freedom of speech as a fundamental right while the French allow restrictions that we wouldn't accept. Is one country right and the other wrong? No, but they're different, and appreciating those differences and understanding the history behind them has helped us understand that no one has all the right answers. It's given us a fresh perspective on our own country and on the world.

Living in France has also changed our attitude towards "stuff." Neither Val nor I is a packrat but our house still seems to have a lot of stuff in it. Our closets are full, our cupboards are full, and there are boxes stacked all over the garage. Where does it come from? Maybe it breeds at night when we're not looking.

But then we go to Provence for months at a time and all we take are three suitcases and Mica. Sure, the houses we rent have dishes and linens and things like that, but we still get by with a lot less than we do in California. And we don't miss all our stuff—in fact, it's liberating to have less to worry about. Feeling that freedom has encouraged us to start getting rid of things, though we still have a long way to go.

Living in France has also made us appreciate America more. We appreciate the convenience of being able to shop when we want to, especially on Sunday. We love the natural optimism of Americans, that sense that we're still living on the frontier and building a new world. And we love the fact that so many people we know, or their parents or grandparents, came from a country far away and made a new life here, adding to the brilliant mosaic of America.

What's the best thing about living in France? The people we've met. It's been by far the best part of our French experience. While we miss the food and the countryside and the *joie de vivre* when we're away from Provence, what we miss most are the friends we've made. We wish we could pack them in our suitcases and bring them back to California with us.

But the biggest thing that living in France has done is bring Val and me even closer. We've always been close and we've always done a lot together, but in France we do pretty much *everything* together. We only have one car, so if we want to go anywhere it's a place we've both agreed on. And we've made friends together—in the US we have "his" and "hers" and "our" friends, but in France every friend is "ours."

Even more than the day-to-day togetherness, *Provence* is something we do together. We started planning for it years ago, first as a vague idea, then slowly filling in the blanks as we went along. Together we decided to quit our jobs and move to another country. Together we've learned a new language and built a new life. Together we've made mistakes and learned to laugh at them and not take ourselves too seriously. It's been a marvelous adventure. Together.

Now we live a bi-national life, shared between two wonderful countries. Sometimes we talk about "home" and ask ourselves whether it's still California or if it's become Provence. We've decided that it's both, because *home is where the heart is* and our hearts are in two places.

Years ago, Val and I took a non-traditional path and our friends and family wondered if we knew what we were doing. Heck, *we* wondered the same thing. It's been scary at times and awkward at times but always, always exhilarating. We've followed our crazy dream through all of its twists and turns and it's enriched our lives beyond measure. And I can't wait to see where it takes us next.

Acknowledgements

My love of travel started early. My parents were both schoolteachers and every summer they would pack up my sister and brother and me, plus the dog and cat, and light out for parts unknown. We would roam around the American West for weeks, camping in state parks and national forests. My desire to explore the world started there and hasn't stopped yet. Thanks Mom and Dad.

This book builds on the adventures I first wrote about in *One Sip at a Time*, a book that would never have been written without the support and encouragement of my friend, the author George Anders. My sincere thanks to George for giving me the confidence to write.

Many people read this book as it was coming together, sharing with me their advice and criticism, and each of them has made it better. My thanks to George Anders, Liam Berryman, Jeff Britting, Rene Haas, Joni Johnson, Elizabeth Mori and my mother Shirley Van Sickle. Special thanks to Elizabeth, who does a remarkable job of helping me see my work through a reader's eyes.

Special thanks also to Jeff, my friend since second grade, who has been my literary comrade-in-arms for half a century.

There are some marvelous online publications devoted to France and to travel and I have the pleasure of writing for several of them. I always appreciate the feedback and criticism I receive because it makes my writing better. I'd like to thank Annette Charlton of *A French Collection*, Janice Chung of *France Travel Tips*, Deb Corbeil of *The Planet D*, Jenny Hughes of *Frenchly*, Carolyne Kauser-Abbott of *Perfectly Provence*, Judy MacMahon of *MyFrenchLife - MaVieFrançaise*, Janine Marsh of *The Good Life France*, and Julie Mautner of *The Provence Post*.

I couldn't live in France the way I do without speaking the language. I owe a great debt of gratitude to my wonderful teachers Gisèle Filiol, Marjorie Hamelin and Malika Labadi—*merci beaucoup chères profs*. And I'd like to give special thanks to my long-time language partner Stéphane Castex and my Bay Area Buddy Joëlle Huet-Ducrot.

As for my friends in Provence, how can I thank them enough? I can't, but I want them to know that I cherish our friendship and that they enrich my life immensely. We really must drink to that!

And finally, I would like to thank my beloved wife Val. Without her I would never have moved to Switzerland, never have moved to France, never have learned French, and never have done any of the things I've written about in this book. Life with Val is a joy, a wonder and a constant adventure, and it gets better every day.

Meet The Author

Keith Van Sickle is the author of the Amazon best-seller *One Sip at a Time: Learning to Live in Provence* and its sequel *Are We French Yet? Keith & Val's Adventures in Provence*. A lifelong traveler who got his first taste of overseas life as a university student in England, Keith later backpacked around the world on his own. But it was the expat assignment to Switzerland that made him fall in love with Europe. With his wife Val and their trusty dog Mica, he now splits his time between California and Provence, delving ever deeper into what makes France so endlessly fascinating.

Keep up with Keith online:

Website: https://keithvansickle.com
Facebook: Keith Van Sickle, Author
Twitter: @keith_vansickle

Read on for a sneak peek at *One Sip at a Time*...

How to Kiss a Frenchman

Viviane, Gérard and André came over for lunch one Saturday. It was a long meal with plenty of courses and plenty of wine, something we were starting to get used to. When they left, Gérard gave me a kiss on each cheek.

People kiss each other all the time in France, as they do in Switzerland, but the rules can vary and we were never sure which set was in play.

The Swiss, as you would expect, are very orderly. Three kisses on the cheeks, left-right-left, no exceptions. People shake hands when they are first introduced but move to kisses as they get to know each other. Women kiss women, women kiss men and men kiss women. Men exchange firm and manly handshakes.

There are clear rules that keep everyone organized. They were probably printed in our village handbook when we lived in Switzerland, right next to the phone numbers for the fire department and the fondue delivery service.

In France it gets more complicated and it varies by region. In Paris it's two kisses. The Parisians also start with the right cheek rather than the left and men don't kiss each other. Parisian men carry man purses, sure, but kissing each other would be a bit much.

When we had stayed in Provence the year before we had started to get into the kissing program. We had discovered that it was three kisses like in Switzerland but the cheek sequence was right-left-right rather than left-right-left. *It is very important to keep this straight.* One of our Swiss friends once had an awkward moment with a French woman. He went left, she went right, and he ended up kissing her on the lips. Quite the international incident.

The other thing about Provence is that men kiss each other. Not all men, but men who are good friends – "*potes.*" The year before, our landlord Pascal gave me the full three-kiss treatment when we left at the end of our stay. I thought it was a warm and friendly gesture but maybe he was just glad to be rid of me.

Here, not far from where we had stayed the year before, it was two kisses rather than three. How were we supposed to know this? Was there a border we had crossed but somehow missed the sign? ("Welcome to Eastern Provence. Please Follow the Local Kissing Regulations. And Enjoy Your Lunch, Especially the Asparagus, Which is Delicious Right Now.")

If you gave three kisses when it should be two, would people think you were rather pushy and forward? If you only gave two kisses instead of three, would you be considered standoffish?

One thing that was consistent across Provence was that men kissed each other. So when Gérard kissed me I wasn't shocked. But I was worried that I might mix up the left-right sequence like my Swiss friend and give him a real kiss. Good thing that didn't happen because Gérard really loved his garlic!

The French Citizenship Test

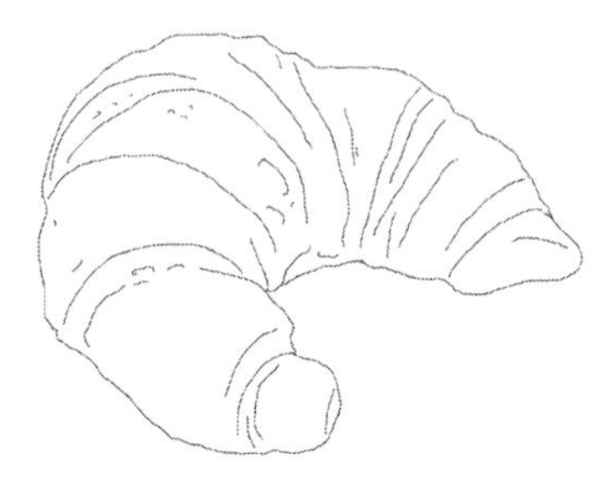

We had croissants for breakfast and as usual we made a mess. They were so flaky that there were crumbs everywhere – on our shirts, the table, the floor, the dog. But when French people ate croissants there was never a crumb in sight. How did they do it? Did they have specially-evolved types of teeth? Were they taught proper crumb-prevention techniques in elementary school? We thought maybe we should invite some of our friends over for brunch and film them with a hidden camera to discover the secret.

This got me to thinking that maybe you had to master proper croissant eating to become a French citizen. I imagined it being part of the rigorous French Citizenship Exam, a multi-day affair.

The first day would be French language, where you would have to write an essay using all 26 (yes, 26) tenses of French verbs.

The second day would be French cultural appreciation, where you would watch a French film and explain what happened. This would be tricky because nothing ever actually happens in French films. You would get extra points for including references to *Man's Fate* or existentialism.

The third day would be French food, where you would be required to match dozens of cheeses with the correct wines, a challenge that even the French would find daunting.

The fourth day would be the driving test, where you would have to find a parking place in Paris in under an hour. Points would be deducted if you ever used your turn signal, something real *Parisiens* never do.

Finally, if you passed all of these tests, you would get to the final exam. They would bring you into a small room and seat you at a table covered with special, highly sensitive crumb detectors. Then a member of the French Immigration Service would bring you the lightest, flakiest croissant imaginable and say, with a menacing smile, "*Bon appétit!*"

Praise for One Sip at a Time

"A delightful collection of vignettes with many laugh-out-loud moments"
Patricia Sands, author of *Drawing Lessons* and *Love in Provence*

"Delightful and engaging!"
K.S.R. Burns, author of *The Paris Effect* and *Paris Ever After*

"Read this book and you'll be smiling for days"
Cris Hammond, author of *From Here to Paris*

"A breezy romp through the tribulations and triumphs of Americans in Provence"
Marjorie Williams, author of *Markets of Provence*

"I loved so many things about this book"
The Good Life France

"The more I read this book, the more I wanted to go back to Provence"
France Travel Tips

"A charming and hilarious book"
Belle Provence Travels

"This one will have you smiling"
Backyard Provence

Available from Amazon

Made in the USA
Middletown, DE
25 January 2019